STEADY NERVES
AND
STOUT HEARTS

The
Enterprise (CV6)
Air Group and
Pearl Harbor,
7 December 1941

Nine SBD-2s and -3s of Scouting SIX over the Pacific on a tactics hop, 27 October 1941. 6-S-14, an SBD-3 (BuNo 4572), nominally assigned to ENS Edward T. Deacon, VS-6's assistant engineering officer, would be shot down by American antiaircraft fire at Pearl on 7 December 1941; 6-S-2, an SBD-2 (BuNo 2175), nominally assigned to VS-6's navigator, ENS Perry L. Teaff, was ultimately lost on 24 February 1942 in a takeoff accident; 6-S-7, an SBD-3 (BuNo 4524), nominally assigned to the squadron engineering officer, LT(jg) Dale Hilton, was shot down at Marcus Island on 4 March 1942. Note non-standard white coding on blue gray background, which was changed to low-contrast black prior to December 1941. (80-G-6678)

STEADY NERVES AND STOUT HEARTS

The
Enterprise (CV6)
Air Group and
Pearl Harbor,
7 December 1941

by Robert J. Cressman &

J. Michael Wenger

PICTORIAL HISTORIES PUBLISHING COMPANY

LIBRARY OF CONGRESS
CARD CATALOG NUMBER 90-60875

ISBN 0-929521-25-0

First Printing: March 1990

Maps & Layout: Robert J. Cressman
Cover Design: Kirk Johnson
Typesetting: Arrow Graphics

About the Authors:

Robert J. Cressman is a historian with the Ships' Histories Branch, Naval Historical Center, Washington, D.C. A graduate of the University of Maryland at College Park (B.A. 1972, M.A. 1978), his publication credits include many articles in magazines, journals and anthologies. His first book, *That Gallant Ship: U.S.S. Yorktown (CV-5)* was published in 1985 by Pictorial Histories.

J. Michael Wenger is a materials analyst with Square D Company in Knightdale, N.C. A graduate of Atlantic Christian College in Wilson, N.C. (BA 1972), he holds an advanced degree from Duke University in Durham, N.C. (MAT 1974). In his avocation as an aviation historian, his publication credits include the Raleigh (N.C.) *News and Observer*, and he was a major contributor to *December 7, 1941: The Day the Japanese Attacked Pearl Harbor* (McGraw Hill, 1988).

PICTORIAL HISTORIES PUBLISHING COMPANY
713 South Third West
Missoula, Montana 59801

Table of Contents

MAPS

INTRODUCTION

In the 48 years since Japanese planes attacked the U.S. Pacific Fleet at Pearl Harbor, many accounts of that event, written from varying viewpoints, have been published. It is not our intention to present yet another overview of what occurred on that day, as the 50th anniversary draws near, nor to debate at whose feet blame rests, but rather examine, in the form of a "small unit history," how that attack affected a certain group of men who suddenly found themselves thrust into a war.

This book began as an article recounting the trials and tribulations of the 36 men (*Enterprise*'s air group commander, his passenger, 13 crews from Scouting Squadron SIX and four from Bombing SIX) who were Pearl-bound on the morning of 7 December 1941. As work progressed, however, we became convinced that, almost without exception, not even the accounts of Pearl Harbor which have emerged in recent years have described accurately the experiences of these men nor have detailed what other operations the carrier *Enterprise* (CV-6) and her air group conducted on that day.

We believe that the narrative which follows is the first to identify the men from *Enterprise* who were in the air that morning in the skies near or over Oahu, and to detail what happened to them. While this story centers on the 36 aforementioned men assigned the a.m. search on 7 December, the Wake Island ferry mission that preceded it and the other operations that occurred on the 7th—the abortive searches for the Japanese fleet and the tragic loss of planes from Fighting Squadron SIX that night—have been included to provide a context for what went on before, and after, that momentous morning.

Robert J. Cressman
J. Michael Wenger
15 June 1989

ACKNOWLEDGMENTS

Dr. Dean C. Allard, Mike Walker, Mrs. Kathy Lloyd, Ms. Regina Akers, Chuck Haberlein, Mrs. Agnes F. Hoover, Mark Weber, John C. Reilly, Jr., James L. Mooney, Raymond A. Mann, Dr. Gary Weir, Ms. Sandra M. Kay, Sylvan M. Dubow, Mrs. Gordon W. Prange, Walter Lord, John Lundstrom, David Aiken, Mark Horan, Richard Frank, James C. Sawruk, Dave Lucabaugh, Dr. Robert L. Scheina, LCDR Maryanne Liberatore, Mrs. Phyllis Freeman, Mrs. Jane Dobson, RADM Wilmer E. Gallaher, CAPT H. Dale Hilton, RADM Wilbur E. Roberts, CAPT Frank A. Patriarca, LCDR Richard H. Best, CAPT Benjamin H. Troemel, CAPT Norman J. Kleiss, CAPT Edward L. Anderson, LCDR John Snowden, LCDR Joseph F. DeLuca, CDR James F. Murray, Audrey G. Coslett, CWO3, Allen Brost, Jack Leaming, Frank Kozelek, J. Lamont Norwood, MAJ John M. Elliot, Dale Sharrick, and Donald H. Jones, Jr.

Special thanks also go to our respective wives and children—Linda Cressman and Mary Ann Wenger, Christine and Robert Cressman, Jr., and Jake and Joel Wenger—who put up with the authors during the lengthy (but necessary) process of research, writing, and rewriting.

DEDICATION

To the memory of Mark Cressman, who, had he lived, would probably enjoy sitting with his daddy, turning the pages of this book and looking at the pictures; and Dr. Gordon W. Prange, not only my mentor at the University of Maryland but a good friend who, like Mark, is missed more than mere words can express.

RJC

PHOTO CREDITS

Most photographs are U.S. Navy official, from the collections of the National Archives and the Naval Imaging Command. Photos marked 80-G can be found at the former, as can the ones marked SC-(Army Signal Corps); the Imaging Command's photos are distinguished by the NH prefix. Photos loaned or given by individuals are indicated by the person's last name.

GLOSSARY

USN/JAPANESE AIRCRAFT NAMES

The U.S. Navy, by and large, did not often use the popular nicknames approved in October 1941 for its naval aircraft, while the Japanese Navy designated its types of planes in a very particular way; the text uses "popular names" sparingly, particularly the Japanese, since those most often applied to enemy aircraft were not even adopted until November 1942.

USN
Grumman F4F-3 -3A "Wildcat"
Douglas SBD-2, -3 "Dauntless"
Douglas TBD-1 "Devastator"
Consolidated PBY-5 "Catalina"
Curtiss SOC-3 "Seagull"
Vought SB2U-3 "Vindicator"
Vought OS2U-3 "Kingfisher"

JAPANESE
Aichi D3A1 Type 99 carrier bomber
(*kanbaku*) ("Val")
Mitsubishi A6M2 Type 00 carrier fighter
(*kansen*) ("Zero")
Nakajima B5N2 Type 97 carrier attack plane
(*kanko*) ("Kate")

JAPANESE NAMES
Will be rendered as in Western fashion, for ease of the reader, with the surname last and the given name first.

Miscellaneous Terms and Abbreviations

A-V(N), USNR: aviation officer holding the designation as naval aviator, qualified for general duty afloat or ashore.
BuNo: Bureau Number
CAP: Combat Air Patrol
CARDIV: Carrier Division
CEAG: Commander, *Enterprise* Air Group
ChC: Chaplain Corps
CINCUS/CINCPAC: Commander in Chief, United States Fleet
Commander in Chief, Pacific Fleet
CO: Commanding Officer
COMAIRBATFOR: Commander, Aircraft, Battle Force
COMCRUDIV: Commander, Cruiser Division
COMDESBATFOR: Commander, Destroyers, Battle Force
COM 14: Commandant, 14th Naval District
COMPATWING: Commander, Patrol Wing
Condition II: A state of readiness wherein a surprise attack may take place at any time by planes, surface ships, or submarines.
Condition III: A state of readiness in which the probabilities of attack are remote, and the crew stands regular peacetime watches.
CTF: Commander, Task Force
CXAM-1: Air Search Radar
D-V(G), USNR: Deck officer, commissioned or warranted . . . qualified for general detail afloat or ashore.
LSO: Landing Signal Officer
MAG: Marine Aircraft Group
MC: Medical Corps
NAS: Naval Air Station
TF: Task Force
T.H.: Territory of Hawaii
USCG: United States Coast Guard
USMC: United States Marine Corps
USN: United States Navy
USNA: United States Naval Academy
USNR: United States Naval Reserve
XO: Executive Officer
YE: Homing Signal Transmitter
ZB: Homing Signal Receiver

Ship Types

AD: Destroyer Tender
AG: Miscellaneous Auxiliary
AKS: General Issue Storeship
AM: Minesweeper
AO: Fleet Oiler
APD: High Speed Transport
AT: Fleet Tug
AV: Seaplane Tender
BB: Battleship
CA: Heavy Cruiser
CL: Light Cruiser
CV: Aircraft Carrier
CVE: Aircraft Carrier, Escort
DD: Destroyer
SS: Submarine
ZR: Rigid Airship

Squadrons

VB: Bombing Squadron
VCS: Cruiser Scouting Squadron
VF: Fighting Squadron
VMF: Marine Fighting Squadron
VMSB: Marine Scout-Bombing Squadron
VO: Observation Squadron
VP: Patrol Squadron
VS: Scouting Squadron
VT: Torpedo Squadron

Ranks and Rates

ADM: Admiral
AMM1c/3c: Aviation Machinist's Mate 1st Class/3d Class
AVCDT: Aviation Cadet
CAPT: Captain (USN & USMC)
CDR: Commander
COX: Coxwain
ENS: Ensign
GEN: General
LCDR: Lieutenant Commander
LT: Lieutenant
LTCOL: Lieutenant Colonel (USMC)
LT(jg): Lieutenant (Junior Grade)
PhM1c: Pharmacist's Mate 1st Class
PO1c/2c/3c: Petty Officer 1st Class/2d Class/3d Class (Japanese Navy, Aviation Rate)
PVT: Private
RADM: Rear Admiral
RMC: Chief Radioman
SEA1c: Seaman 1st Class (USN and Japanese Navy)
VADM: Vice Admiral
WO: Warrant Officer (Japanese Navy, Aviation Rate)

NOTE

Unless otherwise specified, all USN ship names will be understood as being preceded by USS (United States Ship); a USN ship's hull number will be used only when it is first used in the course of the work. All times and dates are those observed locally by the ship, unless otherwise specified, and are rendered in "military" fashion (i.e., 1000 for 10:00 a.m., 1300 for 1:00 p.m., etc.).

CHAPTER I

. . . . .

"Steady Nerves and Stout Hearts."

As the midwatch began on 7 December 1941, the ships of Task Force (TF) 8 were laboring at 16 knots through a restless white-capped ocean on a southwesterly course. Neither the flagship, an aircraft carrier, nor the three heavy cruisers and nine destroyers arrayed around her as her protective screen showed any lights.

Those ships had sailed from Pearl Harbor on the morning of 28 November as part of TF 2—consisting of the battleships *Arizona* (BB-39), *Nevada* (BB-36) and *Oklahoma* (BB-37), the aircraft carrier *Enterprise* (CV-6) and a screen of heavy cruisers and destroyers—under VADM William F. Halsey, Jr., COMAIRBATFOR. Most of the officers and men believed that they were about to engage in intertype training in the Hawaiian Operating Area, as called for in TF 2's quarterly employment schedule, upon completion of which they were slated to return to Pearl on 5 December for the usual post-exercise leave and upkeep.

These men-of-war had put to sea amidst growing international tension, as the United States and Japan stood at an impasse over the situation in the Far East. The two nations had been at odds since the Japanese had invaded China in July 1937 and had occupied Indochina in September 1940, moves which the United States had opposed. Neither side appeared willing to back down in the negotiations then underway between the two Pacific powers.

Having broken the Japanese diplomatic code, though, the United States had gleaned enough information from message traffic by late November 1941 to indicate a potential imminent breakdown of the talks between the two countries, and the possibility of hostilities. Acting on that intelligence, ADM Harold R. Stark, the Chief of Naval Operations, and GEN George C. Marshall, Chief of Staff of the Army, sent a "war warning" on 27 November to their respective commands on Oahu, indicating an unusually tense situation. ADM Husband E. Kimmel, CINCUS/CINCPAC, concerned over the inadequate defenses at his outlying Pacific bases at that critical juncture, directed that VADM Halsey—with

whom he had shared the "war warning" message on 27 November—move planes to "meet emergency requirements . . . at Wake and Midway."

As Halsey was leaving Kimmel's office on the 27th, he asked his Naval Academy classmate how far he (Kimmel) wanted him to go in carrying out his mission. "Goddamn it," Kimmel replied, "use your common sense." As Halsey wrote later: "I think that was as fine an order as a subordinate ever received . . . he had given me full authority as man on the spot to handle the situation as I saw it and that he would back me up to the hilt."

Since the use of army planes had been ruled out—in order to not strip the defenses of Oahu—marine aircraft had to be substituted. *Enterprise* was to ferry 12 Grumman F4F-3s of VMF-211 to Wake Island; *Lexington* (CV-2), in TF 12, was to take 18 Vought SB2U-3s of VMSB-231 to Midway. Before *Enterprise* sailed on the 28th, she hoisted on board two Army P-40s to be flown off as a test—this type of aircraft having been originally considered for duty on those islands. The carrier edged away from alongside Ten-Ten Dock shortly after 0730 and out into the channel; steering various courses and speeds to clear the harbor, she passed channel buoy no. 1 abeam to starboard at 0840 and stood out, joined soon thereafter by *Ellet* (DD-398) and *Fanning* (DD-385), her plane guards.

Enterprise went to flight quarters at 0930, and launched the two P-40s to fly back to Oahu. A half hour later, at 1000, when out of sight of land, Halsey, with the carrier, three heavy cruisers and nine destroyers designated as TF 8, detached the balance of TF 2, including the battleships, to carry out their scheduled intertype tactics and advanced antiaircraft battle practice; the latter stood off to the east under RADM Milo F. Draemel, COMDESBATFOR.[1]

Enterprise then recovered her air group—minus

---

1. These ships returned to Pearl Harbor on schedule, on 5 December, and the three battleships moored to quays at Ford Island—*Oklahoma* alongside *Maryland* (BB-46); *Arizona* and *Nevada* each moored singly. *Arizona* brought the repair ship *Vestal* (AR-4) alongside on 6 December to commence a tender availability.

Aerial view of a portion of the Pearl Harbor Navy Yard, taken at 1100, 26 November 1941, showing *Enterprise* moored alongside Ten-Ten Dock. Had she arrived back at Pearl from Wake on 6 December 1941 as scheduled, she would have been lying there when the Japanese hit on the 7th. (NH, via Walker)

VADM William F. Halsey, Jr., COMAIRBATFOR, *circa* 1941. A USNA classmate once wrote of Halsey (who was known at that time as "Willie," or "Pudge") when he was a naval cadet that his face resembled a "figurehead of Neptune." (NH 95552)

Enterprise's CO, CAPT George Dominic Murray, USNA 1911, with CAPT Lord Louis Mountbatten on board *Enterprise*, 25 September 1941. (USN)

one VF-6 "Wildcat" (its engine refused to start and the pilot, LT(jg) Eric Allen, had had to "hitch" a ride in a TBD from VT-6)—and VMF-211, whose eleven light-gray aircraft contrasted markedly with the *Enterprise* planes whose upper surfaces had already been camouflaged in blue gray some time before. Originally scheduled to take a dozen F4F-3s to Wake, VMF-211 came on board with only 11 because starter trouble had grounded one at Ford Island, and it had to be left behind, its pilot—like Eric Allen—catching a ride to the ship in a Torpedo SIX TBD-1. To enable the marines to carry out their mission, Halsey soon diverted an F4F-3 from VF-6 to give them the 12 they needed. At that point, VADM Halsey and his chief of staff, CDR Miles R. Browning, knew where they were bound; of the pilots of VMF-211, only MAJ Paul Putnam, USMC, and his XO, CAPT Henry T. Elrod, USMC, knew of TF 8's ultimate destination.

As the task force left Oahu in its wake, it went to Condition III, ammunition in ready stowage and depth charges ready for use. Destroyers were to have the full allowance of torpedoes ready for war shot. From *Enterprise* blinked the signal: CURRENT OPERATIONS INVOLVE NECESSITY READINESS FOR INSTANT ACTION. The ships Halsey had available to him at that juncture are listed below:

TASK FORCE EIGHT
(VADM William F. Halsey, Jr., in *Enterprise*)
Enterprise (CV-6) (Flagship)
Enterprise Air Group
(VB-6, VF-6, VS-6, VT-6)
(VMF-211*)

Northampton (CA-26)
RADM Raymond A. Spruance, COMCRUDIV FIVE, in *Northampton*
Chester (CA-27) *Salt Lake City* (CA-24)
McCall (DD-400) *Ellet* (DD-398) *Benham* (DD-397)
Craven (DD-382) *Dunlap* (DD-384) *Fanning* (DD-385)
Maury (DD-401) *Gridley* (DD-380) *Balch* (DD-363)

*Embarked for transportation/ferry to Wake Island

At noon, the ships began heading west. A little over three hours later, at 1512, *Enterprise* commenced the launch of four SBDs for inner anti-submarine patrol close in to TF 8, with a dozen SBDs to search ahead of the ship, from the south-southwest to the north-northwest, out to 150 miles. Midway through this first period of patrols, *McCall* sighted what looked like a mine, or a dummy mine, and destroyed it with gunfire. *Enterprise* later recovered her planes between 1709 and 1718; none had made any contacts.

For *Enterprise*, the voyage had begun with VADM Halsey directing the carrier's CO, CAPT George D. Murray, to issue "Battle Order No. 1" that left no question in anyone's mind about the conditions under which TF 8 would operate, and set the tone for the voyage.

At Sea,
November 28, 1941

BATTLE ORDER NUMBER ONE

1. The *Enterprise* is now operating under war conditions.
2. At any time, day or night, we must be ready for instant action.
3. Hostile submarines may be encountered.
4. The importance of every officer and man being specially alert and vigilant while on watch at his battle station must be fully realized by all hands.
5. The failure of one man to carry out his assigned task promptly, particularly the lookouts, those manning the batteries, and all those on watch on deck might result in great loss of life or even the loss of the ship.
6. The Captain is confident all hands will prove equal to any emergency that may develop.
7. It is part of the tradition of the Navy that, when put to the test, all hands keep cool, keep their heads, and FIGHT.
8. Steady nerves and stout hearts are needed now.

G.D. MURRAY
Captain, U.S. Navy
Commanding

Approved: November 28, 1941
W.F. HALSEY
Vice Admiral, U.S. Navy
Commander Aircraft, Battle Force

Halsey's operations officer, CDR William H. Buracker, confronted his boss with a copy of the order, and the brief exchange that followed probably mirrored the thoughts of many a man on board *Enterprise* that day:

"Admiral, did you authorize this thing?"
"Yes."
"Do you realize this means war?"
"Yes."
"Goddammit, Admiral, you can't start a private war of your own! Who's going to take the responsibility?"
"I'll take it!" Halsey shot back. "Shoot first and

we'll argue afterwards."

While the "Battle Order" set the tone for the overall operation, a memorandum for supervisors and deck watch officers over the signature of CDR Thomas P. Jeter, *Enterprise*'s XO, set forth the practical methods for carrying it out. The normal condition of readiness for the Air Department would be flight quarters or Condition III. Four fighters were to be retained in Condition II from daylight to sunset; one dive bomber in Condition II with two depth charges loaded. All aircraft were to be loaded to capacity with free and fixed gun ammunition. Bombs in the magazines would be in ready condition; torpedoes would have warheads in ready condition in torpedo storage. Every plane that departed the ship was to carry three beanbag-type containers into which messages could be inserted, to be dropped on the carrier's flight deck and thus preserve radio silence. Aircraft sighting any submarine would first make a low pass ("zoom" it), then drop a float light, then open fire with machine guns, resorting to the radio as a last resort "ONLY in case it is evident that no surface vessel's attention has been attracted."

Fire control for the ship's battery would be in Condition III, with ready ammunition to include 50 rounds per 5-inch gun, 20 clips with 160 rounds per barrel for the 1.1-inch battery, and 1,000 rounds per barrel for the .50-caliber machine guns. Ships and aircraft of the task force would observe strict radio silence except for contacts; they would report merchantmen by message drops. Watch officers were standing watch-in-three (three watch sections alternating the duty) in radar plot, with the CXAM-1 manned continuously and operated, at prescribed intervals, day and night. Ship control was to be in Condition III, with lookouts inspected at least once in each watch to make sure each man was familiar with his assigned sector. Control officers were to make sure that each battery officer understood his assigned sector, and the location of friendly ships within those sectors. The officer of the deck was to maintain current familiarity with recognition signals and challenges. The supervisor of the watch, officer of the deck and junior officer of the deck were to keep themselves abreast of the current disposition and positions of the ships therein. The order lastly specified that any floating object "whose character is in any way uncertain" was to be avoided. The memorandum warned that mines might be secured to "dummy periscopes, water-logged boats, or to wreckage or other objects, or they may be tethered in pairs to floating objects."

Halsey's "shoot first . . . argue afterwards" orders made some of the junior officers uneasy. ENS Benjamin H. Troemel, A-V(N), USNR, heard one of his shipmates gasp, "This kind of stuff could start a war!" With all of the play in the papers given to the goodwill mission of Japanese envoy Saburo Kurusu, would the bombing of a submarine mean war? Those who read the front page of the morning Honolulu *Advertiser* on 28 November would have seen a small headline telling of Japan's studying Secretary of State Cordell Hull's "final stand" in the peace negotiations between the United States and Japan. The afternoon edition of the Honolulu *Star-Bulletin* contained much the same ominous tidings: "Next Peace Step Up to Japan." Both papers carried a small notice on the front page that told of the Army forces of the Hawaiian Department being put on alert—itself another product of the "war warning" sent by the Navy and War Departments to their Hawaiian commands.

Enterprise's fighter pilots soon learned that their temporary marine shipmates possessed between 15 and 20 hours in the Grumman F4F-3 "Wildcat," having just made the transition from Grumman F3F-2 biplanes. Furthermore, these had been their first carrier landings in "Wildcats," and they had done little gunnery or bombing in them. Fighting SIX's diarist lamented how VMF-211's skipper had wanted VF-6 to teach his men how to fly F4Fs. "Wish we knew," the diarist commented. Furthermore, VF-6's scribe felt that, while the marines were good, "a dozen of them seems kind of light to take on the whole Jap air force."

Enterprise's air department, meanwhile, pitched in to ready the marines' F4F-3s for their ferry flight. Once during the next few days, LT Richard H. Best, Bombing SIX's XO, heard someone remark in the wardroom, "You'd think Putnam was going to fight the war all by himself," as he scrounged "all of the portable gear that he could from Fighting SIX to improve his spares at Wake."

Several of the younger pilots in VB-6 sought out Best in his stateroom, 0209, the first night out. How would he carry out these "shoot first" orders? The 31-year-old Dick Best, who had been a fighter pilot (VF-2B in *Lexington*, 1935-1938), responded that he would "attack on sight." He evinced understandable uneasiness at the read-between-the-lines nature of the orders. He told his anxious audience, though, that if he shot down the snooper he would not confess to doing it upon his return. He did not intend to be the man who started the Pacific War. "In six months when it was discovered," he reasoned, "I would either be dead or so great a war hero that no one could touch me."

On 29 November, the day that Halsey informed the task force of its destination, saw more routine searches and inner air patrols with, again, no contacts. That morning, Halsey signaled his force and specified the routine his ships would follow as they carried out their mission: they were to "go to general quarters one hour prior to sunrise to remain until sunrise and from sunset to one hour after sunset . . ." "Unless otherwise noted," COMAIRBATFOR's war diary declares, "this procedure will be followed throughout this force until [the] mission is completed . . ." That night, ENS James G. Daniels, III, of VF-6, wrote in his diary: "We learned today that we are taking the marines to Wake Island to support the Patrol group there—sure glad I can stay aboard this bucket." LT(jg) Wilmer E. "Swede" Rawie's diary entry for the 29th reflected the more routine nature of their deployment: "All day steaming westward—in Condition II—and living under very bored conditions in the ready room." Condition II for VF-6 meant a rotation of four manned Grummans, engines warm, ready to take off at a moment's notice.

It wasn't until 30 November that the search planes found anything other than clouds and whitecaps. The morning launch plan called for 14 SBDs to scour the areas that lay from the south-southeast to the north-northwest to a distance of 150 miles. Areas of reduced visibility lay ahead of TF 8, which at that point was steaming through the Pacific beneath partly cloudy skies. On board *Enterprise*, LT(jg) James S. Gray, Fighting SIX's flight officer, was giving gunnery lessons to the VMF-211 pilots, while ENS John C. Kelley, VF-6's navigation and communications officer, and the custodian of the squadron's confidential publications, sought to impart to the marines recognition silhouettes of Japanese aircraft. The latest "dope," though, showed only fixed-gear types, "and on the face of it," Fighting SIX's diarist writes, ". . . either obsolete or optimistic." To Jim Daniels of Fighting SIX, the future enemy looked "not too hot. Equipment slow and fairly obsolescent." Air department painters, meanwhile, were painting the marines' F4F-3s "war color"—the upper surfaces camouflaged with nonspecular blue gray, as *Enterprise*'s planes were.

Meanwhile, on the search, LT(jg) Jack Blitch of Bombing SIX spotted *Narwhal* (SS-167) at 0718 and, about a half hour later, *Dolphin* (SS-169), at 0747, each proceeding back to Pearl Harbor after simulated war patrols in the vicinity of Wake. Blitch saw the ships from about 10 miles away, but found it necessary to descend to 100 feet to make positive identification. Noting that neither ship carried numbers to identify them, Blitch also reported (by message drop, to preserve radio silence) that neither sub apparently knew recognition signals. "When I challenged them," he reported, "they came back with 'This is the U.S.S. *Narwhal* . . . go ahead. . . .'"

Later that same day, at 2127, *Enterprise*'s radar picked up two planes to the east-northeast of TF 8, flying at 32,000 and 50,000 yards away at an altitude of 2,500 feet. The planes disappeared from the radar screen less than 25 minutes later, going off the screen to the northeast, 66,000 yards away. These were, as COMAIRBATFOR's war diarist speculated, "undoubtedly U.S. patrol planes enroute from Johnston to Midway." Two squadrons of PBYs (VP-21 and VP-22), operating from Johnston, Midway, and Wake, were indeed in the area, covering TF 8's route, with orders to keep a lookout for enemy forces that could threaten the mission.

That night, life went on about as usual on board *Enterprise*, with her officers and men spending their leisure time in much the same fashion as they had for some time. Reflecting in his diary on a poker game that had been played earlier, Jim Daniels noted that "Tommy (ENS Lloyd Thomas, A-V(N), USNR, of Torpedo SIX) won all the money." Wil Rawie, having apparently kept in touch with world news on the radio, reflected on the international situation: "This Jap bird Kurusu arrived in the states—Our answer should have been to shoot him and declare war because as I see it—the campaign in the Pacific was launched about today—the dirty dogs . . .".[2]

On Monday, 1 December, beneath partly cloudy skies, *Enterprise* launched three scouts at 0550 for an inner air patrol and 14 to search ahead of the ship out to 200 miles. At 0900, she launched an additional six SBDs for a special inner air patrol to cover the task force while it fueled. The first scouts, meanwhile, came back on board. While they had made no contacts, they had taken note of the effectiveness (or lack of it) of the camouflage of TF 8's ships: pilots reported that the cruisers with light gray paint (*Chester*, in Measure 2, and *Salt Lake City* in light gray with a prominent false bow wave) "are visible at approximately twice the distance of 40 miles, looking down sun." *Enterprise*, on the other hand, being dark gray (Measure 1), could not be seen beyond 15.

At 0920, TF 8 turned into the wind and slowed to seven knots; over the next few hours, *Enterprise* provided fuel oil to *McCall*, *Fanning* and *Balch*; *Northampton* to *Dunlap* and *Benham*; *Salt Lake City* to *Ellet* and *Craven*; and *Chester* to *Gridley* and *Maury*. By 1507, the fueling was completed, but *Northampton* reported that during the evolution a hawser had fouled her number one shaft and propeller, and

2. Rawie was not far from the truth, as we shall see that a Japanese task force, formed around six fleet carriers, had sailed from Hittokapu Bay, in the remote Kurile Islands, on 26 November (25 November east of the International Date Line), bound for Pearl Harbor.

Enterprise underway at sea, late 1941, in Measure 1 system camouflage—dark gray (5-D) with light gray (5-L) tops. This is one of the very few views of this ship at this stage of her career. (USN)

Enterprise's hangar deck ("polished and glossy like a dark grey, unused ice rink," as one *Enterprise* officer recalled), looking aft, *circa* November 1941. Note unmarked Douglas TBD-1 triced up in the overhead, with a Douglas SBD immediately aft. Sailors are wearing the two styles of uniform commonly used in the Fleet at that time, the short "skivvy" whites and dungarees.
(Halsey Collection, NHF)

Aviation metalsmiths work on a Grumman F4F-3 "Wildcat" (coded 3-F-14 and bearing VF-3's "Felix the Cat" insignia) on *Enterprise*'s hangar deck, 28 October 1941. One ex-VF-3 "Wildcat," 3-F-15, would be flown by a VF-6 pilot on 7 December 1941. Among the planes triced-up in the overhead is 2-S-18, a Douglas SBD-3 (BuNo 4565) which "Dusty" Kleiss would fly on 7 December. (80-G-17425)

Pilots sprint to their planes spotted aft on *Enterprise*'s flight deck circa November 1941. The man emerging from the door at left carries a chart board under his left arm. Plane number 10 (R) was nominally assigned to ENS John C. "Butch" Kelly, VF-6's navigation/communication officer. (Halsey Collection, NHF)

Part of the *Enterprise* Air Group on deck, *circa* November 1941, showing SBDs in foreground, TBD-1s in background. Barely visible in the stark shadows in left foreground is LT Earl Gallaher's 6-S-10; 6-S-12 at right was nominally assigned to ENS William P. "Willy" West, A-V(N), USNR. (Halsey Collection, NHF)

The intricate ballet of the flight deck, *circa* November 1941, TBD-1s from VT-6 spotted for takeoff. Six-Tare-Five, (foreground, R) was nominally assigned to ENS John P. Gray, VT-6's assistant personnel officer. Note sailor at left foreground holding up chalkboard with last-minute information for the pilot. (Halsey Collection, NHF)

signaled that it would take about two hours to clear it. Detaching *Benham* to stand by the hobbled heavy cruiser, Halsey ordered TF 8 to steer to the west-southwest and increase speed to 18 knots. During the fueling operations, at noon, the admiral received a coded message from COM 14 that neither *Enterprise*'s nor *Northampton*'s cryptanalysts could break down.

Crossing the International Date Line at midnight meant that 2 December 1941 disappeared ("This is the day that wasn't there," Rawie noted in his diary) and became the 3d. *Northampton* and *Benham* rejoined the formation at 0430, having been picked up by *Chester*'s radar at 0204, shortly after lookouts had spotted them visually. At 0605, *Enterprise* turned into the wind and commenced the first flight operations of the day: three SBDs for the first inner anti-submarine patrol and 14 SBDs to search ahead of the ship from the south-southwest to the northwest out to 200 miles. She launched a second anti-sub patrol at 0940, and recovered the first patrol and the scouts commencing at 1004, the pilots reporting no contacts. They had found the flying weather good, partly cloudy with an unlimited ceiling, moderate winds and a calm sea, and reported a slight haze, but good visibility. Shortly after noon, lookouts spotted a PBY to port, "part of the Wake Island patrol." The second 200-mile search initiated that afternoon, like the morning's, netted no contacts.

That afternoon, on the eve of his departure, MAJ Putnam wrote the CO of MAG-21, LTCOL Claude Larkin, and reflected on the previous days' events. He noted that VADM Halsey had made it plain at the outset that he would spare nothing to see that the marines got off with 12 airplanes in as fine a condition as possible. "All hands aboard have continuously vied with each other to see who could do the most for me. I feel a bit like a fatted calf being groomed for whatever it is that happens to fatted calves . . ." He also noted Halsey's apparent determination "to maintain secrecy regarding the position and activity of this Force," telling of the continuous inner air patrol during daylight, and a full squadron making a search to the front and flanks each morning and evening. "They are armed to the teeth and the orders are to attack any Japanese vessel or aircraft on sight in order to prevent the discovery of this Force." He also reflected on his vague orders, which only told him to do what was "appropriate" upon his arrival. Putnam then asked jokingly: "What's the price on starting a war these days?"

At 0530 on 4 December, *Enterprise* commenced launch of four F4Fs for the first combat air patrol, followed by three SBDs to serve as the inner anti-submarine patrol. Fourteen SBDs were soon airborne to search out to a distance of 225 miles, from the south to the northwest. Shortly after 0700, when lookouts spotted a PBY orbiting the formation—sent out from Wake to guide the marines in—*Enterprise* commenced launching VMF-211; Commander, *Enterprise* Air Group (CEAG), LCDR Howard L. Young, was to accompany the flight in his SBD-2; six additional SBDs were added as escort for the marines. Fourteen TBDs from Torpedo SIX soon lumbered down the deck and took off to act as a second search, covering the sector ranging from the north-northeast to the south-southeast out to a distance of 175 miles. The 12 F4F-3s of VMF-211 then circled the ship as the SBDs proceeded on ahead; *Enterprise* then signaled the PBY to escort the fighters to Wake. At 0730, they set out in that direction. The flagship's radar indicated (erroneously, as it turned out) that the SBDs had rendezvoused with the Wake-bound marines 30 miles from the ship. The carrier then launched four additional F4Fs for CAP duties overhead, and three more SBDs for the inner anti-submarine patrol, to relieve the planes already on station. The morning search landed back on board between 0917 and 0925, within a half hour of the first CAP and inner anti-sub patrols landing, and reported only seeing two contacts in the course of their flight: Wake Island and a PBY. Weather had been partly cloudy, but with an unlimited ceiling and good visibility.[3]

At 0935 on 4 December, during the course of his escort flight, though, ENS Walter M. Willis, A-V(N), USNR, in 6-S-15, spotted three small ships in column 80 miles to the east-northeast of Wake. Encountering LT(jg) H. Dale Hilton on the way back, he joined up and indicated a sighting. Hilton's radio-gunner, Jack Leaming, RM2c, and Willis's radioman, Magee, patted their heads in the codes used by the rear-seaters, and exchanged information in this fashion. The two pilots then headed where Willis believed he saw the ships. They saw nothing, and headed back. Hilton appreciated Willis' concern—what with Battle Order No. 1 in force—but he had encountered hazy conditions similar to this before, when one could imagine seeing almost anything. Hilton remembered that he had once nearly reported French Frigate Shoals as a ship!

Willis, however, a square-jawed ex-marine, stuck

---

3. The gallant story of VMF-211 in the defense of Wake is well-known. The initial Japanese air raid on the island on 8 December (7 December east of the International Date Line) destroyed most of the F4F-3s on the ground. Eventually, the number of "Wildcats" dwindled to none, and the pilots—those who remained—became infantrymen. MAJ Putnam's XO, CAPT Elrod, earned a posthumous Medal of Honor during Wake's defense (8-23 December 1941), for his actions both in the air and on the ground.

pugnaciously to his story—he HAD seen the ships. The escort flight returned on board between 1138 and 1144, and Willis reported his sighting. Apparently, some of his shipmates did not believe him. Fighting SIX's diarist, for example, noted skeptically: "Voight [sic] says he saw a large fleet at the end of his scouting leg, but it was hazy, so he isn't sure..." Other than two VS-6 pilots making "deferred forced landings" on board, the rest of the day passed uneventfully, and the afternoon search reported no contacts.

The "three small ships in column" Willis sighted were the fleet tug *Sonoma* (AT-12), that had departed Wake Island a few days before, and two Pan American Airways (PAA) barges in tow astern. Armed with nothing heavier than .30-caliber machine guns, *Sonoma* plodded toward Honolulu with her cumbersome charges, making only four knots across the far from tranquil Pacific.

That night, "Swede" Rawie recounted the day's events: "Hurrah—we fly—3 hour combat air patrol with orders to *shoot*. Imagine the spree with 1800 rounds of 50 cal. The Marines got off for Wake, tho—God bless 'em—gave one of 'em my bottle of scotch—bet he puts that to good use . . ." Fighting SIX's diarist sighed with relief that the marines had been delivered without incident: "All landed okay," he wrote, "and now let's get the hell out of here before they decide to leave us. All hands agreed that this is no place for a plane with no armor plate and no self-sealing gas tanks. We'll be a lot braver about this war talk when that stuff comes—if it comes..."

At 0500 on the 5th, as TF 8 entered a rain squall, lookouts spotted lights to the southeast. Halsey ordered *McCall*, then screening *Salt Lake City*, to investigate what he believed to be *Sonoma*, which his search had spotted the previous day. Four and a half hours later, the destroyer rejoined the formation, and reported that the strange vessel turned out to be, in fact, the venerable little tug and the PAA barges.[4]

In the meantime, *Enterprise* had launched three fighters and 14 TBDs between 0533 and 0545, the former for inner air patrol and the latter to search the fan-shaped sector from roughly north-northeast to southeast by south, out to 200 miles. She launched a second group of planes (three fighters for inner air patrol and 30 SBDs for searches) between 0904 and 0912. She recovered the first patrol and the TBDs between 0914 and 0928, shortly before *McCall* returned. Fighting SIX's XO, LT Frank Corbin, provided a little zest to the morning's flight operations

when he came in for a landing without his tail hook. Reporting that he could not get it down to land, Corbin waited until *Enterprise* worked up to 20 knots. With 47 knots of relative wind over the deck, Corbin came in with no trouble.

That afternoon, more flight operations ensued—more inner air patrols by VF-6 and a second 200-mile search by VT-6. A few hours after landing the fourth patrol and the scouts that day, the weather began to worsen, with the wind and sea increasing in intensity to a moderate gale. Observed Jim Daniels: "Heading back to Pearl into the Wind—the Destroyers in company are taking an awful beating—It looks like the North Atlantic instead of the Blue Pacific." That evening, on the hangar deck, the men watched *A Yank in the R.A.F.*, starring Tyrone Power and Betty Grable—the first time that movies had been shown on board since the departure from Pearl. An hour before midnight, the task force slowed to 15 knots in the teeth of the storm.

The same high winds and undesirable flying conditions prevalent late on the 5th resulted in cancellation of morning flight operations on the 6th. At 0845, LCDR Hallsted L. Hopping, the CO of Scouting SIX, in 6-S-1, was to have been launched for Pearl Harbor. ENS John H.L. Vogt, Jr., A-V(N), USNR, in 6-S-3, was to accompany Hopping with LCDR Bromfield B. Nichol, COMAIRBATFOR's tactical officer, as his passenger. Nichol was to have reported orally to ADM Kimmel of the completion of the Wake ferry mission. The high winds and heavy seas also postponed the fueling of the destroyers, and pushed back the time of arrival at Pearl Harbor from the afternoon of 6 December to the following morning. Observed a Fighting SIX pilot, "It's raining and rough as hell. This blow is probably making a lot of the girls sick on the *Lurline*"—the Matson liner that had departed Honolulu at noon on 5 December with several wives of *Enterprise* pilots on board.

It was not until about an hour into the afternoon watch (1256) that the weather permitted a resumption of flight operations, *Enterprise* commencing launch at that time of six fighters for an inner air patrol and 14 TBDs to search the sector that lay ahead of the ship from the north-northeast to the south-southeast, out to a distance of 150 miles. Meanwhile, the wind having moderated to a fresh breeze, the heavy ships commenced fueling the "small boys." *Enterprise* fueled *McCall*, *Salt Lake City* fueled *Ellet*, *Northampton* fueled *Benham* and *Chester* fueled *Craven*, steaming into the wind through the heavy seas. Having slowed to seven knots at the outset of the operation, the task force increased speed to 15 upon completion of it, *Enterprise* recover-

4. *Sonoma* eventually reached Honolulu safely, with her tows, on 15 December 1941.

ing the F4Fs of the inner air patrol and the TBDs of the scouting flight. A Torpedo SIX pilot reported sighting *Lexington* and her task force—bound for Midway—two heavy cruisers and five destroyers, at 1345. That night, *Enterprise*'s officers and men watched Gary Cooper in *Sergeant York* (a "4.0 picture"). Reflecting on the film fare of the previous evening, VF-6's diarist observed, (They) "Certainly are priming us full of war movies..." Jim Daniels' diary reflected his disappointment that the return to Pearl had had to be delayed. "Sure hope I get home soon," he wrote, "I'm sick of this cruise." After lamenting that he hadn't even gotten his flight time in yet, he wrote: "Damn. We don't fly in till tomorrow."

The weather had begun to clear, though, as the men of *Enterprise*'s air department and squadrons began stirring at 0400 on 7 December 1941 to get ready for the morning search. Fifteen minutes later, mess attendants served an early breakfast for 24 enlisted men and 30 officers; shortly before 0500, the men assigned to air plot, the ready room talkers and elevator operators, all manned their stations.

General Quarters sounded at 0525. VADM Halsey arrived on the flag bridge soon thereafter.

Some 250 miles due west of Oahu, *Enterprise* swung into the wind at 0615, and commenced launching planes within a few minutes: the CEAG's Douglas SBD-2, 13 SBD-2s and -3s of Scouting SIX, with four SBD-2s and -3s of Bombing SIX, none of which were equipped with armor or self-sealing gasoline tanks. For defensive purposes, each plane shipped a single .30 cal. machine gun in the rear cockpit for the radioman/passenger; depending on the model (SBD-2 or -3), each plane carried two forward-firing .30 or .50 caliber machine guns. None of the planes carried bombs.

The mission given the men who took off commencing at 0618 was to search ahead of the ship from the northeast to the southeast, out to a distance of 150 miles. Upon completion of its search, each section was to turn for Oahu, and land at Ford Island, at NAS Pearl Harbor. The last plane lifted off the flight deck at 0629.

Enterprise fuels *McCall* (DD-400), 6 December 1941. An evolution such as this required expert seamanship, and could be seriously hampered by heavy seas—such as those which prevented the heavy ships of TF 8 from fueling the destroyers en route back to Oahu from Wake. (80-G-21014-B)

TASK ORGANIZATION A.M. SEARCH
7 December 1941

PLANE NO. (BuNo, where known)	PILOT/PASSENGER	SECTOR DEGREES, TRUE
CEAG (BuNo 2162)	LCDR Young/LCDR Nichol	085-095
6-S-2 (BuNo 2175)	ENS Teaff/Jinks, RM3c	085-095
6-S-1 (BuNo 4522)*	LCDR Hopping/Thomas, RM1c	095-105
6-S-3 (BuNo 2160)	ENS Vogt/Pierce, RM3c	095-105
6-S-4 (BuNo 4570)*	LT Dickinson/Miller, RM1c	105-115
6-S-9 (BuNo 2158)	ENS McCarthy/Cohn, RM3c	105-115
6-S-7 (BuNo 4524)	LT(jg) Hilton/Leaming, RM2c	115-125
6-B-5 (BuNo 2169)	ENS Kroeger/Chapman, RM2c	115-125
6-S-11	ENS Fogg/Dennis, RM3c	125-135
6-S-8	ENS Dobson/Hoss, RM3c	125-135
6-S-10*	LT Gallaher/Merritt, RM1c	075-085
6-S-5	ENS West/Hansen, RM3c	075-085
6-S-16 (BuNo 4521)	LT(jg) Patriarca/DeLuca, RM1c	065-075
6-S-15 (BuNo 2159)	ENS Willis/Ducolon, COX	065-075
6-S-14 (BuNo 4572)	ENS Deacon/Coslett, RM3c	055-065
6-B-9 (BuNo 2184)	ENS Roberts/Jones, AMM1c	055-065
6-B-3 (BuNo 2181)	ENS Gonzalez/Kozelek, RM3c	045-055
6-B-12	ENS Weber/Keaney, SEA1c	045-055

*Indicates equipped with ZB ("Zed Baker") homing gear.

Necessity had dictated two changes to Scouting SIX's tactical organization for the flight, with Bombing SIX providing the necessary men and machines. ENS Earl R. Donnell's plane, Six-Sail-Eighteen, was given a "down" and Donnell's place was taken by ENS Edwin J. Kroeger in 6-B-5. Likewise, ENS Troemel discovered that the aircraft assigned him for the flight, 6-S-17 (BuNo 2170), had a fouled spark plug. Troemel, a licensed third mate with the Cuba Mail Steamship Line and the Army Transport Service before he had joined the Navy and undergone flight training, ruefully reflected that this was the only time since he had come on board *Enterprise* that he had had to abort a take-off. ENS Wilber E. "Bill" Roberts, in 6-B-9, who had only expected to sit in his plane on the flight deck as a stand-by, replaced him. Two additional Bombing Six planes had been assigned to the flight as well. ENS Manuel Gonzalez, A-V(N), USNR, learning who had been scheduled to fly the morning search, had approached LT(jg) Edward L. "Andy" Anderson, and offered to trade places with him. Anderson, whose wife did not reside on Oahu, and knowing that "Manny's" wife did, agreed readily to the swap. Jo Dene Gonzalez, however, had sailed for the West Coast, along with several other VB-6 wives, at noon on 5 December on board *Lurline*.

Ironically, other pilots, who had been launched a short time before, were also setting a course for Pearl. Unlike the *Enterprise* planes, the aircraft they flew carried bombs or torpedoes; their wings and fuselages bore the red sun insignia of Japan. They came from the six aircraft carriers of the 1st Air Fleet, that had sailed from the remote Kurile Islands on 26 November (25 November east of the International Date Line). This powerful task force steamed undetected across the North Pacific to reach a launch point north of Oahu. The paths of some of the men flying the Japanese planes and most of the men flying the SBDs would soon intersect in the partly cloudy skies above Oahu. The Japanese expected a fight; the Americans did not.

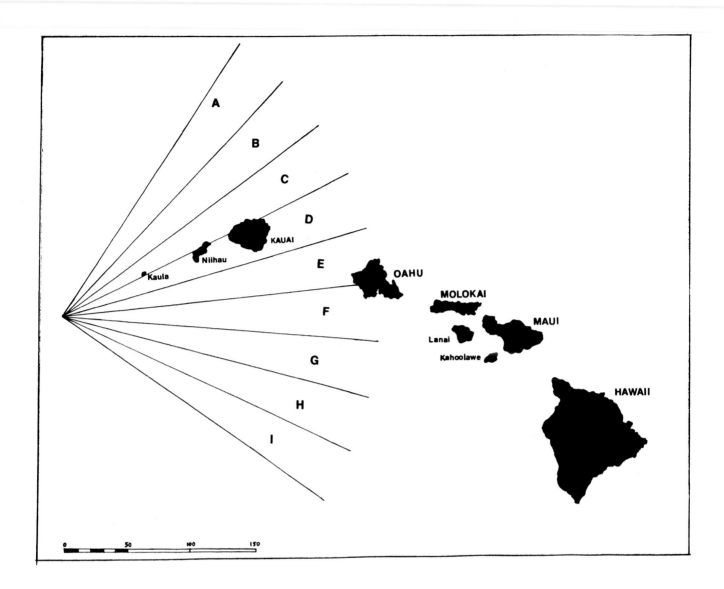

Hawaiian Islands, with Search Sectors for the a.m.
Scouting Flight on 7 December 1941.

Key to Search Pattern Sectors A-I
(All Pilots/Crew from VS-6
Unless Otherwise Noted)

A   ENS Gonzalez/Kozelek, RM3c (VB-6)
    ENS Weber/Keaney, SEA1c (VB-6)

B   ENS Deacon/Coslett, RM3c
    ENS Roberts/Jones, AMM1c (VB-6)

C   LT(jg) Patriarca/DeLuca, RM1c
    ENS Willis/Ducolon, COX

D   LT Gallaher/Merritt, RM1c
    ENS West/Hansen, RM3c

E   LCDR Young/LCDR Nichol (CEAG)
    ENS Teaff/Jinks, RM3c

F   LCDR Hopping/Thomas, RM1c
    ENS Vogt/Pierce, RM3c

G   LT Dickinson/Miller, RM1c
    ENS McCarthy/Cohn, RM3c

H   LT(jg) Hilton/Leaming, RM2c
    ENS Kroeger/Chapman, RM2c (VB-6)

I   ENS Fogg/Dennis, RM3c
    ENS Dobson/Hoss, RM3c

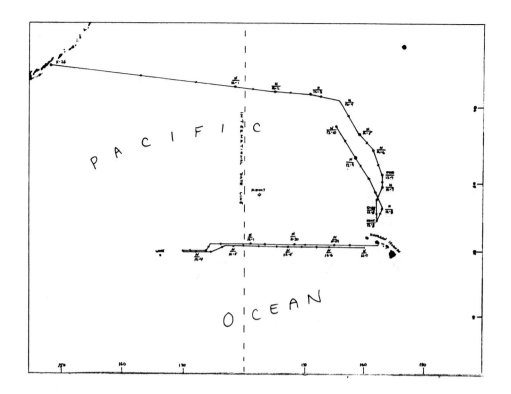

Movements of the Japanese First Air Fleet (Pearl Harbor Attack Force) and Task Force EIGHT, November-December 1941.

Times for the Japanese force (Upper) are reckoned by Tokyo Time, which is 19½ hours later than Hawaiian time. Times for TF 8 are those observed locally by the task force. All positions are for noon, unless otherwise noted. (Adapted from Chart in *Hawai Sakusen* and *Enterprise* Deck Logs)

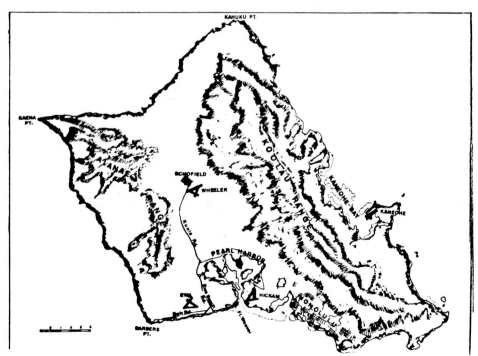

Map of Oahu, T.H., identifying key installations, geographical landmarks and roads mentioned in the course of the book.

LCDR Hallsted L. Hopping (L), CO of Scouting SIX, chats with LCDR Howard L. Young (R), *Enterprise*'s Air Group Commander, at a picnic on Oahu *circa* October 1941. (Coslett)

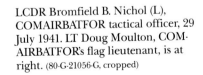

LT(jg) "Dusty" Kleiss appears to be dressed in comparatively formal fashion (note tie) in relation to his more casually-attired shipmates: ENS "Willy" West at barbeque; others present include (R-L) LCDR Hopping, LCDR Young (eating) and LT Wilmer E. Gallaher, VS-6's XO. (DeLuca)

LCDR Bromfield B. Nichol (L), COMAIRBATFOR tactical officer, 29 July 1941. LT Doug Moulton, COMAIRBATFOR's flag lieutenant, is at right. (80-G-21056-G, cropped)

CHAPTER II

· · · · ·

"*I Hope You Won't Get Me Wet Today, Sir...*"

The men in the Douglas SBDs that began fanning out in their respective search sectors—unaware of the Japanese planes flying toward Oahu—reflected the diversity of the Navy and the nation it served. The most experienced pilot on the search was the air group commander, LCDR Howard L. Young, who flew the uniquely marked SBD-2 set aside for his use.

The Brooklyn-born Young had just turned 40 years old on 23 November. A graduate of the USNA Class of 1923, the wiry, blue-eyed pilot had had three nicknames bestowed on him at various times in his career at the Academy: "Brigham" for the Mormon pioneer, "Cy" for the baseball hurler of the era, and "Hal." By 1941, *Enterprise* pilots apparently used only one: "Brigham." Like many naval officers of his era, his first tour of duty afloat was in a battleship, *Florida* (BB-30). He then served at the Naval Torpedo Station, Newport, R.I, and then in a destroyer, *Sturtevant* (DD-240), before he took flight training at Pensacola, winning his wings in 1926. Service in *Langley* (CV-1) in VO-2 and VF-2 followed, before he underwent training at NAS Lakehurst, New Jersey. He then joined the aviation unit of the rigid airship *Akron* (ZR-4), making one of the first hook-ons to the airship's unique "trapeze" recovery installation, and after *Akron*'s loss served in the aviation unit of *Macon* (ZR-5). A succession of sea duty followed, in VCS-12 on board *Tuscaloosa* (CA-37), and VB-2 in *Saratoga* (CV-3) before he became officer-in-charge of the Experimental Division, Operations Department, NAS Norfolk, a billet in which he served for two years until he joined Fighting SIX in June 1939. In April 1941, he became CEAG, and in time, became known affectionately as "a prince of a guy . . . [who] looked after his people."

LCDR Bromfield B. Nichol, VADM Halsey's tactical officer, to whom COMAIRBATFOR had entrusted the task of personally reporting the completed Wake ferry mission directly to CINCPAC/CINCUS headquarters, occupied Young's back seat.

A graduate of the USNA Class of 1924, Nichol, 37, was a classmate of Scouting SIX's CO, LCDR Hopping. A tour of duty in the battleship *Mississippi* (BB-41) had preceded his getting his wings at Pensacola in 1926. He then served in torpedo and scouting squadrons attached to the seaplane tender *Wright* (AV-1) before he served successive tours as flight instructor at NAS Norfolk, in a scouting squadron based in the heavy cruiser *Louisville* (CA-28), and as a squadron XO at Pensacola. Assigned to Bombing SIX in January 1938, he joined the staff of COMCARDIV ONE, then-RADM Halsey, soon thereafter.

Young's wingman—ENS Perry L. Teaff, a bright, witty 25-year old Oklahoman—had earned his bachelor's degree from State Teacher's College, Springfield, Mo., before being appointed AVCDT in April 1938. Winning his wings at Pensacola in July 1939, Teaff had requested, and gotten, duty on a "West Coast carrier." A superb and daring pilot, he had joined Scouting SIX soon thereafter, and became known, in time, as the squadron "character" who possessed a fine sense of humor. Teaff's radioman, a quiet, serious, good-natured 22-year-old Texan, Edgar P. Jinks, RM3c, was, as his shipmate A. G. Coslett recalled, "like myself, a shorttimer in the Navy, but liked it."

The next senior pilot was the skipper of Scouting SIX, LCDR Hopping. The 39-year-old New Yorker had graduated in the USNA Class of 1924 and then served a two-year tour in the light cruiser *Richmond* (CL-9). Following aviation instruction, he won his wings at Pensacola in 1927. Over the years that followed, "Spike" Hopping (as he had been known at the academy) flew torpedo planes, flying boats, and scouts, from such ships as *Langley*, *Ranger* (CV-4), *New Orleans* (CA-32) and *Concord* (CL-10). Becoming CO of Scouting SIX on 10 July 1941, Hopping, a big, rangy man regarded highly by his men as a tactical genius, drove his squadron hard to prepare them for whatever might lie ahead. Socially, his junior officers remembered him as "gracious," and as one who "really cared about his officers and men." Harold "R" Thomas, RM1c, 35 years old and the squadron's leading radio-gunner, was Hopping's radio-gunner in Six-Sail-One on the morning of 7 December. Some who served under Thomas considered him "a hell of a good guy," who would sometimes kid the younger men about their mistakes and work to help them to not make them again, "always trying to help," others remembered him as a serious-natured, mature radioman who'd "been around a long time."

Hopping's wingman that morning was ENS Vogt, who had originally been scheduled to take LCDR Nichol to Pearl Harbor the previous day before the weather had caused the flight to be cancelled. A 26-year-old Californian, "Johnny" Vogt had been appointed an AVCDT in January 1939, and won his "wings" in late November of the same year. On 2 February 1940, he had reported to Scouting SIX. An "earnest and hard-working young man," he was also an avid acey-ducey player; he and his roommate, Ben Troemel, often whiled away many off-duty hours in that variant of backgammon. His radioman that morning was an eager, ruddy-faced 19-year-old Texan, Sidney Pierce, RM3c.

LT Clarence E. "Dick" Dickinson had graduated from the USNA in 1934; born in Florida but appointed from North Carolina, Dickinson had just turned 29 six days before. He had served in the heavy cruiser *San Francisco* (CA-38), the destroyer *Phelps* (DD-360) and heavy cruiser *Portland* (CA-33) before he underwent aviation instruction, first at Pensacola and then at Miami, between September 1940 and April 1941, after which time he joined Scouting SIX. Some of the men with whom he shared the wardroom often considered this gangling young man with a long, thin neck and sharp facial features (leading some to call him "Dickie Bird" behind his back) as "excitable."

His radio-gunner, William C. Miller, RM1c, a 20-year-old North Carolinian, had enlisted in 1937 and, following his "boot camp" training at Norfolk, had joined Scouting SIX on 30 September 1938. A big, personable "country boy, tall and lanky with a good ol' farm boy gait," Miller was an excellent radioman, and Dickinson, as VS-6's flight officer, saw to it that the North Carolinian "was in the rear seat every time he flew." On the morning of 7 December, the usually outgoing, imperturbable Miller expressed noticeable uneasiness to Dickinson as the former helped the pilot adjust his radio cord. Noting that his enlistment was nearly up, Miller reflected that out of the 21 men in his radio class, he seemed to be the only one who hadn't suf-

John H.L. Vogt, Jr., *circa* 1938. (USN)

LT Clarence E. "Dick" Dickinson, USN, while an instructor at NAS Corpus Christi, Texas, 1 September 1942. (80-G-17503)

Sidney Pierce (second from right, standing) boxes the ears of one of his shipmates while Johnny Snowden stands at right with a can of Pabst during a VS-6 picnic, *circa* October 1941. (Kleiss)

William C. Miller, RM1c, USN, *circa* 1941. "At all times," LT Dickinson later wrote, "Miller . . . conducted himself in an outstanding manner and in accordance with the best traditions of the Navy. He kept himself alert and cool and in every way successfully carried out his assignment." (USN)

William C. Miller, RM1c (center), in a lighter moment, supported by two Scouting SIX shipmates. (Kleiss)

AVCDT John R. McCarthy, USNR, May 1940. (USN)

AVCDT Manuel Gonzalez, USNR, 1939 (USN)

fered a water landing at one time or another. "Hope you won't get me wet today, sir," Miller drawled seriously.

Dickinson tried to reassure the young man who was soon to finish his enlistment and his tour with VS-6, travel to the West Coast and wed Miss Pauline Walker, his high school sweetheart, as soon as he arrived back on the mainland. Reflecting that it would probably be their last mission together, Dickinson said: "That's all we've got to get by— this morning's flight." Apparently satisfied, Miller clambered into the rear cockpit of Six-Sail-Four.

Dickinson's wingman, ENS John R. McCarthy, A-V(N), USNR (sometimes nicknamed "Charlie" for comedian Edgar Bergen's dummy), hailed from Minnesota, and had graduated from the University of Minnesota, Class of 1939. Appointed AVCDT in September 1939, McCarthy won his wings the following summer and was assigned to Scouting SIX; although junior to Dickinson, he actually possessed more flight experience. McCarthy's rear seat man was black-haired, brown-eyed Mitchell Cohn, RM3c, a 21-year-old New Yorker.

In the next section was LT(jg) H. Dale Hilton, a Los Angeles, Calif., native, 27, who had received a BS degree in engineering from the University of Southern California at Los Angeles in 1936. Enlisting in July 1936, Hilton became an AVCDT in November of that year, and received his ensign's commission in December 1937. Designated a naval aviator at that time, he joined Torpedo FIVE in *Yorktown* (CV-5), and flew Douglas TBD-1s with that squadron until September 1940, when he was assigned to an AVCDT selection board at Long Beach, Calif., a billet in which he served until assigned to Scouting SIX in the summer of 1941. His radioman, Jack Leaming, RM2c, had often flown with Hilton since late October 1941. Leaming had just turned 21 the day before (6 December) and looked forward to celebrating in style when he got back to Oahu. On top of that, his enlistment was up the following Tuesday, 9 December, and he was "mustering out."

Hilton's wingman was not from Scouting SIX but from Bombing SIX, and, among the four pilots from the latter unit involved in the morning's mission, probably possessed the most experience. ENS Edwin J. Kroeger, A-V(N), USNR, graduated from Purdue University in 1937 and had entered the USNR soon thereafter. A football and baseball player in his collegiate days, "Bud" Kroeger had flown gliders at 19, evidencing an early interest in aviation. Appointed a naval aviator in August 1938 after completing his flight training, he had joined Bombing SIX soon thereafter. His rear-seat man was Walter F. Chapman, RM2c.

Scouting SIX picnic, *circa* October 1941. ENS "Willy" West (R), holding a can of Pabst Blue Ribbon beer, munches on a sandwich, while enlisted men mug for the camera. Among them is Mitchell Cohn (third from right), who would be killed in action on 7 December, and Audrey G. Coslett (far left), who would be wounded the same day. (Kleiss)

Leonard J. Kozelek (L) and Audrey G. Coslett (R), "boot camp" classmates, *circa* 1941. (Coslett)

LT (jg) Donald H. Jones, on Guam, 1946. (Jones)

Bombing Squadron SIX pilots, January 1942. Three of these men (marked with *) flew in the a.m. search on 7 December 1941. Front row (L-R): LT Harvey P. Lanham, LT H. A. Smith, LT Richard H. Best (XO), LCDR William R. Hollingsworth (CO), LT John D. Blitch, LT Joe R. Penland, LT James W. McCauley; Rear row (L-R): LT(jg) L. J. Check, ENS J. J. Doherty, ENS Norman F. Vandivier, ENS A. L. Rausch, ENS Tony F. Schneider, ENS Fred T. Weber*, LT(jg) Edwin J. Kroeger*, ENS Delbert W. Halsey, LT(jg) Edward L. Anderson, ENS K. H. Holcomb, LT(jg) John J. Van Buren, ENS Thomas W. Ramsay, ENS C. R. Walters, ENS Wilbur E. Roberts*. (Murray)

The next most experienced Bombing SIX pilot who drew the morning search was ENS Manuel Gonzalez, who had volunteered to take "Andy" Anderson's place. A California native like Hilton and Vogt (born in Compton), Gonzalez, 30, was the oldest of the junior officers on the flight that day. A football and basketball player in his college days at Chico State, Gonzalez stood a shade under 6'2" tall and weighed in at around 200 pounds. He applied for flight training in 1938 and impressed the examining board, who evaluated him as "excellent" officer material and found him to be "frank, engaging, and earnest; quiet, but determined." To the selection board, the cleancut Gonzalez presented an "excellent appearance" and possessed the earmarks of a "fairly aggressive" officer. When he first saw him, one of his shipmates in Bombing SIX likened him to a "big lumbering ox"—an affectionate term, not one of derision. Gentle in speech and nature, he was thought of fondly.

Gonzalez's radioman that morning was Leonard J. Kozelek, RM3c, of Massillon, Ohio—a hard-working and conscientious young man who had just celebrated his 23d birthday on 1 November 1941. Those who knew him best considered him "sensi-

tive and spirited" and someone who loved and enjoyed being with people. He had dropped out of high school to work, and in time developed much skill as a cook. Taken under the wing of the Ohio State Highway Patrol, he prepared special-occasion banquets at the Police Barracks, and the troopers taught him how to work with radios, an interest he pursued in the Navy.

Flying wing on Gonzalez was ENS Frederick T. Weber, A-V(N), USNR, 25, of Des Moines, Iowa. After his collegiate education at Knox College, Galesburg, Ill., he had attended Drake University in Des Moines, and obtained his bachelor's degree in 1938, after which time he enlisted in the USNR. Appointed AVCDT in July 1939, the fun-loving Weber won his wings and was designated a naval aviator in May 1940; he joined Bombing SIX on 12 June 1940. Weber's radio-gunner on the morning of 7 December was 25-year-old Lee E. J. Keaney, SEA1c, of Sandusky, Ohio.

ENS Edward T. Deacon, A-V(N), USNR, of Scouting SIX, drew a Bombing SIX wingman, ENS Wilbur E. "Bill" Roberts, A-V(N), USNR. Deacon, 27, from Bridgeport, Conn., had graduated from the Rensselaer Polytechnic Institute, Troy, N. Y., where he

Pilots of Scouting Squadron SIX, on board *Enterprise circa* 24 January 1942. Those indicated by * had flown the 7 December a.m. search. Front row (L-R) LT(jg) Dale Hilton*, LT Reginald Rutherford (originally assigned to the Asiatic Station for duty, he returned to *Enterprise* on the night of 8 December, his orders rendered uncertain by the outbreak of war), LT Wilmer E. Gallaher (XO)*, LCDR Hallsted L. Hopping (CO)*, LT Clarence E. Dickinson*, LT Frank A. Patriarca*, and LT(jg) Norman J. Kleiss. Rear row (L-R): ENS Percy W. Forman, A-V(N), USNR, ENS William P. West, A-V(N), USNR*, LT(jg) Benjamin H. Troemel, ENS Daniel Seid, ENS Reid W. Stone, A-V(N), USNR, ENS Earl R. Donnell, A-V(N), USNR, LT(jg) J. Norman West, LT(jg) Edward T. Deacon*, ENS Cleo J. Dobson, A-V(N), USNR*, LT(jg) Perry L. Teaff*, LT(jg) Carlton H. Fogg*. Of this group, Hopping, Fogg, Donnell and Seid would be dead within about a week of this photo's being taken, shot down in the Marshalls. (Hilton)

Lee E. J. Keaney, SEA1c, ENS Weber's radiogunner, *circa* January 1942. (Murray)

AVCDT Walter M. Willis, USNR, August 1940 (USN)

had studied to become an architect, a profession he pursued briefly before he began his naval career. Enlisting in the USNR in September 1937, Deacon underwent his initial flight training at New York's Floyd Bennett Field before being commissioned as AVCDT in July 1938. Winning his wings at Pensacola in August 1939, Deacon expressed a desire for "scouting—west coast" upon graduation; he was assigned to Scouting SIX on 14 September 1939, and reported on board the squadron on 2 October 1939. His radio-gunner was gangling 20-year-old Audrey Gerard Coslett, RM3c, a happy, outgoing lad known to his shipmates as Jerry.

Deacon's wingman, ENS Roberts, 26, hailed from Detroit, Mich.; graduating from the University of Michigan with a BS in aeronautical engineering in 1938, he was appointed AVCDT on 26 January 1939, and a naval aviator on 7 February 1940. He joined Bombing SIX soon thereafter. In his rear seat that morning as a passenger sat one of Bomb-

ing SIX's indispensable men, one of the mechanics responsible for keeping the planes flying, Donald H. "Pooky" Jones, AMM1c.

LT(jg) Frank A. "Pat" Patriarca, who had just turned 28 on 3 December, hailed from Providence, R.I., and during his time at the USNA had been known as "congenial and carefree . . . always on the go, looking for some new sphere of action." After graduation in 1937, he had served in the light cruiser *Detroit* (CL-8). Following flight training at Pensacola, he joined Scouting SIX in June 1940. His radioman was Joseph F. DeLuca, RM1c, who, like Leaming and Thomas E. Merritt, RM1c (the latter flying with the squadron XO, LT Gallaher), had joined Scouting SIX from *Enterprise*'s ship's company. DeLuca's shipmates considered him "always a good guy, generous and feisty"; as one of VS-6's senior radiomen, he had the respect which came from his being "very well thought of by everyone in the squadron . . ."

Patriarca's wingman was ENS Willis, who had

Scouting SIX radio-gunners, *circa* January 1942. Those who flew on the a.m. search on 7 December 1941 are indicated by an *. Front row: Jack Leaming, RM2c*, Donald L. Hoff, RM3c*, Alfred R. Stitzelberger, RM3c; John W. Snowden, RM3c; William H. Bergin, RM1c*; Middle Row (L-R): Bailey, AM3c; Joe Cupples, RM1c; Earl E. Howell, RM3c; Thomas E. Merritt, RM1c*; O. L. Dennis, RM3c*; Louis D. Hansen, RM3c*; Rear row (L-R): Porter W. Pixley, RM3c; David B. Craig, RM3c; William H. Stambaugh, RM2c; Joseph F. DeLuca, RM1c*; Harold "R" Thomas, RM1c*; John D. Dance, RM3c; Edgar P. Jinks, RM3c*; Roy L. Hoss, RM3c*. (Kleiss)

sighted the three small ships on 4 December. Willis, 24, a Minneapolis native and former student at the University of Minnesota, had served a hitch in the U.S. Marine Corps before he enlisted in the USNR in October 1939. Some regarded the blue-eyed, brown-haired Walt Willis, who had won his wings at Pensacola in August 1940 and joined Scouting SIX the next month, as one of the best pilots in the squadron. Willis' passenger—like Roberts'—was not a radioman, but the oldest of the enlisted men making the flight that morning, well-liked 36-year-old Fred J. Ducolon, COX, of Davenport, Iowa. Ducolon was the squadron's master-at-arms, a "good-natured guy . . . who enforced squadron regulations with a modicum of humor."

The XO of Scouting SIX, flying Six-Sail-Ten, was LT Wilmer E. Gallaher of Wilmington, Del.; Gallaher, 34, had served in *Arizona* and *Barney* (DD-149) before his flight training at NAS Pensacola (during which time he dated the daughter of the station commandant, then-CAPT William F. Halsey, Jr.) and his winning his wings in 1935. He then served in the *Ranger*-based VF-5 and the *Langley*-based VP-11 before he trained pilots at Pensacola from June 1938 to June 1940. Loyal and dedicated (and regarded by at least one enlisted man as a "cocky son of a gun" and a stickler for regulations), he joined Scouting SIX in June 1940 as flight officer. Occupying his rear seat that morning was "quiet, studious," Thomas E. Merritt, RM1c, another one of Scouting SIX's more experienced radiomen, "a sharp guy in all respects."

Gallaher's wingman was Maryland-born ENS William P. West, A-V(N), USNR, who was one day away from celebrating his 28th birthday. Holder of a B.A. in business administration from the University of Minnesota (June 1938), "Willy" West had been a fraternity man, an all-frat handball champion and a boxer. After college he had enlisted in the USNR, gone to Pensacola as AVCDT, and won his wings in November 1940. Promoted from AVCDT to ENS on 27 November 1940, West received orders to *Enterprise*—his first choice for sea duty—and Scouting SIX that same day. His radioman was Louis D. Hansen, RM3c, a big, raw-boned character from American Falls, Idaho, who was only two weeks away from his 20th birthday. Well-liked by his shipmates, Hansen was competent and quiet; a slow-moving individual, he naturally acquired the nickname "Speed."

The last section, like most of the others, consisted of two VS-6 planes. One was flown by ENS Carlton T. Fogg—a handsome, dashing bachelor regarded as a "prize catch" by the ladies. Twenty-four years old, the tall, gangling Massachusetts native and former chemical engineering major, had graduated from the University of Maine, Class of 1938, had served in VS-2 on board *Saratoga* and in VS-71 as an AVCDT, USNR, and had reported to VS-6 in late September 1939. His radioman was a "jolly, good-natured, easily kidded" 28-year-old Kentuckian, Otis Lee Dennis, RM3c.

Fogg's wingman was big, strapping ENS Cleo J. "Dobby" Dobson, A-V(N), USNR, 23, who, like his good friend Perry Teaff, hailed from Oklahoma. A versatile athlete, "Dobby" had graduated in 1938 from Oklahoma Agricultural and Mechanical College, where he had played football, basketball and baseball. Appointed AVCDT in September 1938, he won his wings at Pensacola in February 1940, and received orders to Scouting SIX soon thereafter. His radio-gunner that morning was L. A. Hoss, RM3c.

Soon after the last plane in the morning search had cleared the bow ramp, *Enterprise* steadied back on her original course and increased speed; landfall on Oahu was still several hours steaming away. As the SBDs took their departure, none of the pilots and passengers probably thought that the flight into Oahu would yield anything more than the clouds and whitecaps that had become familiar sights since the voyage had begun. All of the men were in high spirits—they were headed for home.

Ahead of them, some 250 miles to the east, however, strange things were happening. At 0630, soon after the last SBD had cleared *Enterprise*, the general stores issue ship *Antares* (AKS-3), which had arrived from Canton Island at the entrance to Pearl Harbor with a 500-ton steel barge in tow, summoned the ready-duty destroyer *Ward* (DD-139) to investigate what looked like a small submarine—what proved to be one of five Type A "midget" submersibles launched earlier to reconnoiter Pearl—1,500 yards off her starboard quarter. *Ward*'s officer-of-the-deck asked her captain, LT William W. Outerbridge, to come to the bridge. Throwing on a blue and white Japanese print kimono over his pyjamas, and slipping his feet into bathroom slippers, Bill Outerbridge, only a few days in command of the old destroyer, rushed from his sea cabin. At the same time, on the opposite side of the island of Oahu, ENS William P. Tanner, Jr., A-V(N), USNR, was lifting his PBY-5, 14-P-1 (BuNo 2419) off Kaneohe Bay for a regularly scheduled patrol over the fleet operating areas off Oahu.

At 0640, *Ward* rang down an increase in speed, and, bone-in-teeth, bore down on the submersible, working up to 25 knots. ENS Tanner's PBY arrived on the scene soon thereafter, and sighted a submarine about one mile south of Pearl, with an American destroyer—*Ward*—"close astern." The circumstances put Tanner in a difficult spot—he had orders to bomb any submerged sub outside of its assigned operating area. The sub's conning tower appeared to be awash, and the bow breaking water at short intervals, led the young PBY pilot to believe that the destroyer was escorting an American submarine in distress. Prudently refraining from dropping depth charges, Tanner circled overhead, dropping two float lights to retain contact.

Ward, then at general quarters, fired two shots from her main battery—the first, fired from number one mount, missed, as Tanner could see from his Olympian vantage point overhead in 14-P-1; the second apparently passed clean through the conning tower. As those on board *Ward* watched, the sub heeled to starboard, slowed, and started to sink. The PBY pilot saw the destroyer change course, to avoid running down the sub, and drop depth charges directly in its path. Then certain that *Ward's* quarry was an enemy craft, Tanner maintained his approach and dropped a depth charge slightly ahead of where he believed the sub's bow to be.

Outerbridge sent one message at 0651: WE HAVE DROPPED DEPTH CHARGES UPON SUB OPERATING IN DEFENSIVE SEA AREA, but, knowing that there had been other instances of destroyers dropping depth charges upon suspected "submarine" contacts in the past few months, followed it up by a second at 0653, amplifying his earlier one: WE HAVE ATTACKED FIRED UPON AND DROPPED DEPTH CHARGES UPON SUBMARINE OPERATING IN DEFENSIVE SEA AREA.

ENS Tanner, too, reported the attack, sending a coded transmission at about the same time. COMPATWING ONE requested verification, which Tanner duly sent: SUNK ONE ENEMY SUBMARINE ONE MILE SOUTH [OF] PEARL HARBOR.

Outerbridge's last message reached COM 14's headquarters at 0712, whence LCDR Harold Kaminski, D-V(G), USNR, the duty officer, relayed it to a succession of individuals by telephone. As the minutes passed, more men became aware of *Ward's* action with the submarine in restricted waters.

Meanwhile, two Army privates at the Opana mobile radar site, at Kahuku Point, on Oahu's northern coast, lingered after the prescribed 0700 quitting time to get in more practice with the equipment's oscilliscope. They noticed an unusually large "blip", closing from 136 miles to the north. At 0720, one of the two, PVT Joseph Lockard, telephoned the Air Warning Service information center at Fort Shafter, stressing the fact that the size of the blip reflected "a very large formation of planes." To PVT Joseph P. McDonald, the telephone operator who took the call, the voice from the Opana station seemed "excited."

"Thinking [that] it must be a returning naval patrol, a flight of Hickam bombing planes, or possibly a flight of B-17s from the coast," however, the watch officer in the control center, 1stLT Kermit A. Tyler, of the 78th Pursuit Squadron, "dismissed it as nothing unusual."

CHAPTER III

· · · · ·

"What the Hell Goes On Here?"

The men in the *Enterprise* planes, however, knew nothing of *Ward*'s submarine contact and the large "blip" on the Opana station's 'scope, as a monotonous parade of clouds and whitecaps passed before them. One by one, each two-plane section completed its search and banked in the direction of Pearl, from Gonzalez and Weber in the northernmost sector to Fogg and Dobson in the southernmost. To give their radiomen homing practice, some pilots instructed their rear-seat men to tune in to the Honolulu radio stations—KGMB or KGU—which were providing a veritable homing beacon for the incoming B-17s expected at Hickam Field that morning.

As "Brigham" Young and Perry Teaff neared Oahu, the sight of ships, below, broke the monotony. Shortly after 0720, the two pilots spotted the 20-year-old Atlantic-Richfield Oil Co. tanker, SS *Pat Doheny*, to starboard. She had departed Long Beach on 23 November for Honolulu with a cargo of oil. Flying due east, Young and Teaff noticed two naval vessels around 0730: the submarine *Thresher* (SS-200), returning from a seven-week simulated war patrol in the vicinity of Midway, with a critically injured sailor on board; and the destroyer *Litchfield* (DD-336), the radio-relay vessel for the Pacific Fleet's submarines and carrying a doctor and pharmacist's mate for transfer to the submarine. The two ships had rendezvoused only a short time before and were proceeding back to Pearl. The *Enterprise* fliers had been briefed in the "fly sheet" for the morning's operations that they might encounter *Thresher* during the flight; her medical emergency had resulted in the presence of *Litchfield*.

Meanwhile, as Young and his wingman were overflying the submarine and the destroyer, LCDR Hopping and ENS Vogt came across a ship, too. Hopping spotted her broad on Six-Sail-One's port bow, 20 miles away, and signalled Vogt to "remain outside gun range" while he (Hopping) investigated. Scouting SIX's skipper soon found the vessel to be *Pat Doheny* on her way to Honolulu. Upon checking out the ship's identity, Hopping looked for Vogt,

but, not finding him, completed his sector search alone and headed for Barbers Point.

Enterprise's plan of the day for 7 December had specified that LT John F. Hugues, ChC, the ship's Roman Catholic chaplain, would hear confessions and celebrate early mass in the crew's reception room at 0645. An early breakfast for the ship's company was scheduled for 0700, and a late breakfast for the air department and squadrons at 0745. At 0800, the paravane gear was to be rigged and tested, and all swabs were to be aired in the outboard starboard passage on the main deck. The ship was scheduled to arrive at Pearl Harbor about 1600 and moor at Ten-Ten Dock. The plan of the day sternly warned all hands "not to discuss the recent destination or operation of this Force with any civilian or other person whatever."

For the first time since TF 8 had departed Pearl Harbor, Halsey had left the bridge and his spartan sea cabin to shave and bathe, and put on a clean uniform before relaxing with a "comfortable breakfast." He and his flag secretary, LT H. Douglas Moulton, D-V(G), USNR, were on their second cups of coffee when the telephone rang. "Doug" Moulton answered it, listened for a moment, and then turned to Halsey, telling him that the staff duty officer had just informed him that a message had just arrived, reporting an air raid on Pearl.

"My God," Halsey exclaimed as he sprang to his feet, "they're shooting at our own planes. Get the word to Kimmel!" Since he had not furnished Pearl Harbor with advance notification of the arrival of *Enterprise*'s scouts (radio silence was not to have been lifted until *Enterprise* had arrived at Pearl), Halsey initially assumed a case of mistaken identity. Moments later, though, his communications officer, LCDR Leonard J. "Ham" Dow, arrived with a dispatch, received at 0812, AIR RAID ON PEARL HARBOR X THIS IS NO DRILL, that convinced the admiral that the bad tidings that Moulton had passed on were genuine. In Bombing SIX's ready room, Dick Best heard the talker standing by the

Douglas SBD-2 (BuNo 2162) assigned to the *Enterprise*'s Air Group Commander, 17 October 1941, its special status reflected in its markings, visible more clearly on the original print: COMMANDER *ENTERPRISE* GROUP on the side of the fuselage, ahead of the star. Additional markings CEG are on the cowl, in black, and on the wing root. The rudder appears to have been left in light gray. BuNo 2162 had been in service about seven months to that point, and would be flown by LCDR Howard L. Young (and other pilots) into March 1942. Later assigned to a succession of USMC squadrons, VMSB-231, -232, and, finally -241, it saw combat in the Battle of Midway, and, after a stint with VB-10 and VMSB-233, was removed from the list of operational aircraft ("stricken") on 22 April 1943. (80-G-279380)

A section of SBDs over the Pacific, 17 October 1941: 6-S-13 was nominally assigned to LT(jg) Frank A. Patriarca; 6-S-16 to ENS John Norman West, A-V(N), USNR. The planes flying toward Pearl Harbor on the morning of 7 December were in two-plane elements such as this. (80-G-12435-A)

blackboard suddenly blurt out: "Pearl Harbor has been attacked. This is not—repeat not—a drill!" Pilots exchanged mystified glances. Something was very, very wrong. Unbeknownst to the Oahu-bound *Enterprise* aviators, Japanese planes had unleashed a surprise attack upon the ships of the Pacific Fleet at Pearl Harbor, as well as upon nearby airfields and military installations.

Among the first men from *Enterprise* to encounter the enemy were "Brigham" Young and his wingman. While passing Barbers Point, both Young and Teaff glimpsed what appeared to be a squadron of aircraft wheeling in column over Ewa Mooring Mast Field, the USMC air facility on Oahu. Both thought them to be Army pursuit planes, and Young gave them a wide berth. Descending to 800 feet, the *Enterprise* air group commander and his wingman headed for Ford Island, passing abeam of Ewa to port. At that moment, a solitary plane appeared, pulled up in a wingover, and commenced what looked like a mock run on Teaff's SBD. The Oklahoman, thinking his attacker was an Army pilot, played along and allowed the aircraft, a Mitsubishi A6M2 Type 00 carrier fighter ("Zero"), probably from *Soryu*, to pull within 75 feet of his tail.

Simultaneously, at a point halfway between Ewa and Ford Island, numerous antiaircraft bursts spattering the sky above Pearl caught LCDR Young's attention. Nichol saw the same thing, and mused: "Why in the hell was the Army training on Sunday morning?" Then, he noticed a plane boring in on the two SBDs, but soon dismissed its pilot as a "young and inexperienced" Army flier trying to "flat hat."

The pilot, however, proved to be Japanese, and rendered any speculation as to his identity academic when he opened fire on Young's wingman. At the outset, Perry Teaff thought the "Army" pilot was making a mistake. Almost miraculously, in view of the close range, neither the puzzled pilot nor his radio-gunner was hit; but 7.7-millimeter bullets from the "Zero's" guns passed through the horizontal stabilizer and glanced off the skin of the wings and fuselage.

Having now overtaken his quarry, the Japanese pilot reversed course and began another firing pass on Six-Sail-Two. Teaff, the identity of his assailant now clearly established, countered with a tight turn to the right, while Jinks, who had deftly unshipped the free gun, quickly squeezed off a burst at their tormentor. Sufficiently deterred, the "Zero" pilot left 6-S-2 alone but turned his attention to Young's SBD-2.

The air group commander (perhaps devoutly desiring that he had his regular radio-gunner, John M. O'Brien, CRM, from VF-6, at his back) pushed his plane into violent evasive maneuvers, practically standing it on its nose and then zig-zagging vigorously

as he dove toward Oahu. "For Christ's sake, Brom," Young implored his passenger over the interphone, "GET THE GUN OUT!" Despite some furious fumbling, Nichol, who had probably not had any free gunnery training since Pensacola, could not comply. He did not get the single .30-caliber gun unshipped—perhaps being unfamiliar with the method of releasing the gun from its housing by depressing a pedal with one's foot and then using one's hands to swing the gun into position to fire it. Young had meanwhile charged his fixed guns, but the fastmoving nature of the fight left him no opportunity to use them.

Despite the evasive action taken by each man to shake the "Zero," Young and Teaff remained together, a tribute to their combined and individual skill as pilots. The action, however, had taken them low over a canefield north of Pearl City, a small town on the northwestern shore of Pearl Harbor. While circling this field, Young realized that friendly antiaircraft fire was reaching up at them no matter which way they turned. Thinking that they would not make it back to *Enterprise*, Young knew that his only option was to head for Ford Island.

Roaring in low to attract as little attention as possible, the two pilots dropped their flaps and landing gear, and began their descent through the "damndest amount of antiaircraft fire" that Nichol had ever seen. Young tried to raise the control tower—to no

CAPT James M. Shoemaker, USN, CO, NAS Pearl Harbor. (NH 42305)

Geysers of water cascade skyward from alongside *West Virginia* (BB-48) and *Oklahoma* (BB-37), while smoke (R) boils from the burning seaplane hangars on Ford Island's south end. Torpedoes have already struck *Raleigh* (CL-7) and *Utah* (AG-16) (L). Soon thereafter, *Enterprise*'s pilots began arriving in the vicinity of Pearl. (NH 50930)

As torpedoes strike home on battleships moored on "Battleship Row," alongside Ford Island (background, L), smoke boils skyward from burning hangars at Hickam (foreground, R). (Wenger)

avail. Despite his having made recognition signals, he saw the tracers continue to reach out toward them; as the CEAG later reported, "I was under fire all the way across Oahu and until my wheels touched the ground." At that point, some guns were only 50 yards away! Young's daring landing later elicited the admiring comment from Fighting SIX's diarist: "Nice dodging, 'Brigham'!"

The first person that Young and his passenger met after their SBD-2 had rolled to a stop was CAPT James M. Shoemaker, the CO of NAS Pearl Harbor. Shoemaker, too, had had a busy morning thus far. Dressing in his quarters when the first bombs shattered the Sunday peace, he telephoned the NAS duty officer, LT Frank A. Erickson, USCG, the aviator assigned to the Coast Guard cutter *Taney*, then moored at Honolulu, and demanded: "What the hell kind of drills are you pulling down there?"

Shoemaker hastily threw on his tropical uniform—white shorts, white short-sleeved shirt and sun helmet—and hopped into his Model A Ford. He drove toward a rising column of smoke (burning seaplanes and a hangar) and there assisted in fire-fighting and salvage efforts; leaving those in

good hands he set out in his car to see how his command was fighting back. He picked up a wounded sailor from the capsized target ship *Utah* (AG-16), transported him to an aid station, and was starting back toward the administration building when he caught sight of two planes—Young's and Teaff's, as it turned out—approaching the Luke Field side of the air station. The first landed. Shoemaker drove over to meet it while the second plane—which the captain took to be Japanese, chasing the first in, but which was, in fact, Perry Teaff's—pulled up and away, Teaff braving the maelstrom of metal to make a second pass. Shoemaker found the new arrivals obviously agitated. Fired at by friend and foe alike, it was small wonder that Young and Nichol, as they climbed stiffly out of the *Enterprise* group commander's SBD-2 at about 0825, demanded angrily in almost one voice: "What the hell goes on here?"

Quickly learning of their ordeal, and apprised of their desperate need to get to the Submarine Base, the location of ADM Kimmel's headquarters, Shoemaker drove the two across the field in his Ford, to NAS Landing "A", where he "shoved them

Scene shortly around 0845 showing *California* (BB-46) at left, sinking; smoke in background is from the burning *West Virginia* and *Arizona* (BB-39). Oiler *Neosho* (AO-23), after chopping her mooring lines, has backed away from Berth F-4 at the NAS and is in the channel to the east of Ford Island, having just cleared the capsized *Oklahoma*. "Brigham" Young and his passenger, Brom Nichol, saw a scene similar to this a short time before as they prepared to leave Ford Island for CINCPAC headquarters at the Submarine Base. (80-G-32640)

Ewa Mooring Mast Field, on the morning of 7 December 1941, only moments before Japanese aircraft began their attacks.

off for the Submarine Base in a NAS boat." By that point, refugees from the bombed and torpedoed battleships were arriving there, in "droves," all oily, some wounded, some burned.

The withering barrage from the American guns had meanwhile forced Teaff to make a second approach; thankfully, the gunners possessed more enthusiasm than accuracy for he managed to get down relatively unscathed. Although Young's aircraft had been holed several times, neither the pilot nor his passenger had been hurt. Likewise, Teaff and Jinks, too, happily took stock of the situation that found them still alive and unhurt as well. Their plane, however, had taken hits in the fuselage. The two quickly set to work to fix what damage they could find.

One SBD crew was not as fortunate at the outset. Available evidence indicates that the first Scouting SIX plane shot down by the Japanese may have been Johnny Vogt's. Vogt, as we have seen, had become separated from LCDR Hopping in the time it took Scouting SIX's skipper to scrutinize the plodding *Pat Doheny.* Although MAG-21's "Record of Events" does not mention it, LTCOL Claude A. Larkin, USMC, CO, MAG-21, later testified: "We saw one of these *Enterprise* airplanes and one Japanese airplane collide in the air. Both of them fell and burned a half mile south and east of Ewa." Vogt's SBD-2 crashed near the intersection of Belt Road and Ewa Beach Road; neither Vogt nor Sid Pierce had gotten out. Searching soldiers later found the wreckage of a Japanese plane — perhaps from *Kaga* (whose "Zeroes" had been assigned the task of strafing Ewa Mooring Mast Field) — "in [the] same vicinity," on Belt Road, lending credence to Larkin's claim

of having seen a mid-air collision. While the precise identity of the Japanese pilot whose plane may have collided with Vogt's is not known for certain, two *Kaga* "Zero" pilots, of the nine who took off, failed to return from the first wave: PO2c Seinoshin Sano and PO2c Toru Haneda.[1] Returning *Kaga* pilots claimed one enemy plane shot down and about 20 destroyed on the ground at Ewa.

LT Dickinson and ENS McCarthy probably arrived in the vicinity of Ewa soon after Vogt. They had scoured the search sector assigned them and then set course for Oahu. By 0825, the two were in sight of the island, approaching Barbers Point from the south at 1,500 feet. Dickinson noted splashes in the water off the south coast (improperly fused antiaircraft shells in all probability) and four ships about three miles off the entrance to Pearl, none of which seemed to be firing. Thinking that a Coast Artillery battery had gone berserk on a Sunday morning, Dickinson remarked to Miller: "Just wait! Tomorrow the Army will certainly catch hell for that."

Puzzled, he then peered at "black balls of smoke, thousands of them, changing into ragged fleecy shapes"— antiaircraft bursts over Pearl — but dense smoke over Ewa hampered his efforts to discern what was happening there, as did a towering billow of smoke mushrooming and rolling skyward from "Battleship Row" in the middle of the harbor. At that point, Dickinson could not see any other aircraft, but apparently sensed danger. Motioning

---

1. *Kaga*'s loss in fighter pilots (four) was the highest experienced by any of the six Japanese carriers. *Soryu* lost three, while *Hiryu* and *Akagi* lost one apiece.

McCarthy alongside, he led his section to an altitude of 4,000 feet above Barbers Point.

At that moment, the two SBDs attracted the attention of Mitsubishi A6M2 Type 00 carrier fighter pilots from the 2d *Chutai* of the aircraft carrier *Soryu*: WO Hakaru Tanaka, PO3c Kyoichiro Hagino and SEA1c Isao Doikawa of the 2d *Shotai* and PO1c Mitsuomi Noda and PO2c Kaname Yoshimatsu of the 3d *Shotai*, part of the 1st Wave Fighter Unit assigned combat air patrol over Ewa, covering *Kaga*'s fighters as they worked over the field.

The latter pair singled out McCarthy's 6-S-9, astern of Dickinson. Both SBDs roared earthward in a 3,000-foot dive, trying to shake their pursuers, but only succeeded in running into the 2d *Shotai*. The "Zeroes'" bullets and shells set fire to McCarthy's plane, and flames streamed back from the right side of the engine and from the right main fuel tank. Although dropping further behind his section leader, McCarthy continued doggedly taking evasive action, circling to the left. After fighting his ship as long as he could, he fought his way free of his cockpit and bailed out. His parachute blossomed open at barely 200 feet. Mitchell Cohn, either already dead or, due to the cramped conditions of the rear cockpit of an SBD, unable to get free as the plane screamed earthward, remained on board as 6-S-9 crashed one mile off Ewa's southwest runway, near Ewa Beach, and burned beyond salvage. McCarthy landed in a tree, and when he tried to climb down, fell and broke his leg.

The five "Zeroes," meanwhile, all pounced on the lone SBD-3. Miller, having swiftly unlimbered the single .30-caliber Browning, bravely tried to keep the enemy at bay. Wounded once, he reported that he had scored hits on one of their tormentors. Expending the last of his ammunition, Miller then said that he had been hit again. Glancing over his shoulder, Dickinson thought he saw one Japanese plane falling—but wasn't sure. An instant later, he heard his gallant gunner let out a blood-curdling scream over the interphone. Dickinson then squeezed off two bursts at a "Zero" that crossed ahead of him, but sensed that the SBD-3, its left wing tank afire and control cables shot away, was going into a spin at 1,000 feet. He shouted for his radioman to bail out; hearing no answer, he leaned out of the cockpit and propelled himself out into the inside of the spin, free of the burning "Dauntless." The slipstream ripped the goggles from his face.

Men on board *Pyro* (AE-1), moored to a dock in West Loch, unknowingly witnessed the end of the unequal contest between the *Soryu* fighters and the VS-6 section, when, at 0832, they saw what they believed to be two "enemy" planes "crash and burst into flames in the direction [of] Barber's [sic] Point." Some of the ammunition ship's sailors saw the two pilots descending by parachute.

The victor over McCarthy and Dickinson may have been SEA1c Doikawa, who claimed three aerial victories that morning upon his return to *Soryu*. He also almost certainly flew the plane Miller claimed to have hit, as his A6M2 was the only fighter of the 2d or 3d *Shotai* to be damaged.

"Zeroes" seemed to be everywhere. LT(jg) Patriarca and ENS Willis arrived in the vicinity of Barbers Point at about 0825 and started to make their approach to Pearl. Patriarca noticed, however, the smoke rising

Three VS-6 "Dauntlesses" in formation, *circa* November 1941. The SBD at top is equipped with a smoke-generating tank beneath the belly of the aircraft, and what looks like a 100-pound bomb beneath the port wing, a practice bomb rack beneath the starboard. 6-S-4 (R), an SBD-3 (BuNo 4570) was flown by LT "Dick" Dickinson on 7 December 1941. The planes are painted in blue gray upper surfaces, light gray lower; markings are in low-contrast black. Note single-mount .30 caliber machine guns in rear cockpits. (Halsey Collection, NHF)

Tangled wreckage of ENS Vogt's SBD-2 (BuNo 2160), one block off Belt Road, Ewa Beach Road, 26 December 1941. (USN)

Tail of ENS "Charlie" McCarthy's SBD-2 (BuNo 2158), 26 December 1941. (USN)

Wright R-1820 engine from LT Dickinson's SBD-3, 26 December 1941. The stencilled card reads NAVY CRASH 7 DEC. 1941 INVESTIGATION COMPLETED DO NOT REMOVE THIS SIGN. (USN)

Burnt and twisted wreckage are all that remains of the SBD-3 (BuNo 4570) flown by LT Dickinson on 7 December. This view was taken by crash investigators, 26 December 1941. (USN)

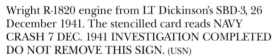

from over Ewa, and many planes in the air. The two SBDs continued eastward, following the southern coast of Oahu, Patriarca's radioman, DeLuca, alertly pointing out antiaircraft fire over Pearl Harbor, as well as splashes rising from the waters south of the harbor entrance channel— probably unexploded antiaircraft shells plunging into the sea. At that instant, red tracers flew past Six-Sail-Sixteen; simultaneously, the morning sun glinted off the red *hinomaru* of a plane as it banked over Ewa.

Several "Zeroes" made firing passes on Patriarca and Willis from above and behind, as things began

An Aichi D3A1 Type 99 car-rier bomber takes off, *circa* Spring, 1942. White fuse-lage band indicates assign-ment to the carrier *Shokaku*, while the white stripe on the fin and rudder reflects the markings of a *shotaicho*, or *shotai* (section) leader. Type 99s from *Shokaku* shot down ENS "Manny" Gon-zalez of Bombing SIX and his radioman, Leonard J. Kozelek, RM3c, about 0833 on 7 December. (Wenger)

with formation flying, had instructed his radioman to tune in to KGU (the NBC affiliate known as "The Voice of Hawaii") for homing practice as they neared Oahu, perhaps to the strains of "Plantation Airs" or the "Friendly Gospel Hour." About 25 miles from the coast, Weber sighted what looked like Army aircraft at about 3,500 feet, and watched them for several minutes, not cognizant of the fact that what he saw was part of the First Wave Strike Unit from the Japanese 5th Carrier Division (*Shokaku* and *Zuikaku*) rendezvousing about ten miles from Kaena Point to return to their ships.

Some of *Shokaku*'s returning pilots, flying Aichi

happening "too damn fast." Patriarca pushed his SBD-3P into a steep diving turn, heading for the coastline with throttle pushed to the stop, while DeLuca turned in his seat to unship the single .30-caliber Browning. At the same time, Patriarca opened up on the radio that Japanese planes were attacking the island of Oahu and not to acknowledge the transmission; after evading the "Zeroes," he shaped a course back to the ship using the 0600 Point Option, but only then realized that Willis was no longer with him. Ducolon may not have even unshipped the gun to fight off the "Zeroes"; the last glimpse DeLuca had of Ducolon was of the squadron's master-at-arms still facing forward in his seat in 6-S-13's rear cockpit. No trace of Six-Sail-Thirteen, nor of its crew, was ever found.

A similar fate befell the sole Bombing SIX section of the morning search. ENS Gonzalez and ENS Weber had, like the others, seen nothing but white-caps and clouds in the course of the flight. Flying 500 feet above and 500 yards to starboard of his section leader, Weber, who had from time to time in his tour with Bombing SIX experienced difficulty

D3A1 Type 99 carrier bombers, most likely sighted the Americans about 0830 and then turned towards them. "Manny" Gonzalez probably watched the planes approaching, and, like his shipmates else-where that morning, thought them to be U.S. Ar-my. Seeing tracers reaching toward him from sup-posedly friendly planes, Gonzalez called out on his radio at about 0833: THIS IS 6-B-3, AN AMERICAN PLANE. DO NOT SHOOT. Then came a second transmission from Gonzalez as he instructed Kozelek over the interphone: STAND BY TO GET OUT THE RUBBER BOAT. *Shokaku*'s action report infers that Gonzalez may have put up a stout defense: "Six car-rier bombers fought an enemy two-seated plane at the rendezvous point, and shot it down." No trace of the big, personable ensign and his well-liked radioman was ever found. Gonzalez' death pro-foundly saddened Dick Best; he felt the loss of the "big, lumbering" "Manny" Gonzalez more than any other. Jim Murray, RM1c, the squadron's leading radioman, felt "heartbroken" at Kozelek's death. Both men would be missed.

Fred Weber and Lee Keaney in Six-Baker-Twelve,

who had apparently drifted far enough away so that 6-B-3 had disappeared from view, however, knew nothing of Gonzalez's mortal combat, his transmission having gone unheard by his wingman, whose radio was tuned to KGU. Turning his attention away from the aircraft rendezvousing to starboard, Weber noticed that his section leader was nowhere to be found.

Banking his SBD around in a wide turn, scanning the sky for 6-B-3, Weber made numerous "S" turns that failed to yield any sign of Gonzalez until he spotted a lone plane flying at his original altitude and heading. Pushing the throttle forward to catch up, he pulled to within 2,000 yards of the aircraft ahead of him when it suddenly reversed course toward him. The ensign made an easy turn to join up with the other plane—which appeared to be doing likewise—when the supposedly friendly plane turned aggressively toward him, and revealed the red *hinomaru* on its port wingtip. Weber pointed the SBD's nose down at full throttle, roaring down in a steep dive toward the ocean, pulling out only 25 feet above the whitecaps, racing away from immediate danger and perhaps the fate that had befallen his section leader. After he had instructed

Keaney to switch from KGU to ship's frequency—and only then learned of the Japanese raid on Pearl Harbor—Weber set course for Barbers Point.

LT Gallaher and ENS West had, to that point, enjoyed an uneventful search, with the exception of West's discovering that he had an inoperative radio battery and generator. With the remaining operating radio on board 6-S-10, Gallaher instructed Merritt to home in on KGU. Then, as they neared Oahu, both pilots noted ten planes off their port bow, rendezvousing at about 1,000 to 1,500 feet. The two SBDs passed about 500 feet beneath the strange aircraft, each pilot assuming that the planes above were U.S. Army. Continuing the flight, Gallaher had Merritt shift back to ship's frequency,

"Old Glory" still flying from her flagstaff, *Arizona* lies shattered at her berth on 7 December 1941. *Tennessee* (BB-43), moored just ahead, plays water on the surface of the harbor to keep burning oil from engulfing her, while *West Virginia* lies outboard of *Tennessee*. *Arizona* had been Earl Gallaher's first ship upon graduation from the Naval Academy. He vowed "to get the guys that did this," and made good on that vow at the Battle of Midway. (80-G-32424)

shortly before arriving near Barbers Point around 0830. Suddenly, disquieting radio traffic came into Gallaher's and Merritt's earphones: "Pat" Patriarca's familiar voice, and then "Manny" Gonzalez's. With a dead radio, West and his rear-seat man, "Speed" Hansen, of course heard nothing; smoke rolling out to sea in the vicinity of Barbers Point caught West's attention but did not alarm him. He assumed that the fires came from sugar cane fields being burned to clear the land—not uncommon on Oahu. Only when Gallaher and his wingman viewed Ewa Field and Pearl Harbor did the awful truth dawn on them. Gallaher would later learn that at the base of one of the columns of oily black smoke lay *Arizona*, the first ship he had served in after graduation from the USNA and one for which he held much affection.

Another pilot approaching Barbers Point shortly after 0830 was LCDR Hopping, who, as we have seen, had become separated from ENS Vogt. At that moment, Gonzalez's identifying message crackled into his earphones. Alerted, Hopping looked toward Ewa, and what he saw prompted him to broadcast a report that Pearl Harbor was under attack by Japanese aircraft. Opting for a landing at Ford Island, as Young and Teaff had done, Hopping braved the heavy antiaircraft fire, and set down at about 0845, 20 minutes after the arrival of the CEAG and his wingman, and just ahead of the second wave of Japanese dive bombers. After landing, Hopping taxied to the control tower to arrange to obtain bombs for his plane and any others that happened to make it to Ford Island, as well as to inform COM-AIRBATFOR of events on Oahu. With the tower transmitter inoperative, Hopping returned to Six-Sail-One and, several times, broadcast the "details of the attack, and that Ford Island Field was usable"—the latter providing one "consoling thought" on board *Enterprise* amidst a welter of disturbing ones. At that time, Chief Gunner William M. Coles, from the air station, showed up and agreed to get bombs for the three SBDs on the field "and for others which might arrive later."

ENSs Deacon and Roberts had had the search sector immediately to the south of the one scoured by Gonzalez and Weber; as they neared Oahu at about 0820, Roberts sighted a loose formation of approximately 30 planes flying on a course roughly north, about 100 feet above the whitecaps. The two pilots observed them to be painted green and assumed them to be Army aircraft. Roberts, however, noted odd insignia—red "meatballs"—and thought how stupid it was for the Army "to paint their planes like that for war games—someone might take them for Japanese!" Coslett noted the red spot on the

fuselage of one of the strange aircraft and remarked to his pilot: "It looks like the Army's changed the markings on their planes."

Despite the 400 yards that lay between them, the American and Japanese planes droned toward their respective destinations, each making no effort to challenge the other. What the men in the SBDs did not know was that they were encountering a group of Nakajima B5N2 Type 97 carrier attack planes—hence the dark coloration—from the 1st and 2d Carrier Divisions (*Kaga* and *Akagi*; *Soryu* and *Hiryu*) that had just wrought havoc on the battleships at Pearl Harbor. Roberts saw one plane approaching them head-on, but at a slightly lower altitude, and squinted into his telescopic sight. Drawing a bead on the green-painted *kanko*, he thought "how good a target it would make if it were . . . enemy." At that moment, the stranger rocked his wings; Roberts did likewise. The tension thus dissipated, both SBDs continued on course to Barbers Point. Coslett could almost taste that cold can of Primo beer that lay ahead.

As they had reached their destination at about 0830, they first noticed smoke rising from the vicinity of Pearl Harbor, as well as geysers of water off Oahu's south coast. Canefield fires? Commonplace. Geysers of water? No. Something funny was going on. In 6-S-14, Coslett changed radio frequencies so that they could communicate with the tower at Ford Island and request landing instructions but soon discovered "that there was no such thing as circuit control, everyone was trying to transmit voice messages with utter disregard for anyone." Around 0833, both pilots and their rear-seat men heard the transmissions from Six-Baker-Three (Gonzalez) that caused the pieces to fall into place. Deacon told Coslett to "mount the machine gun, load it, and stand by."

Deacon and Roberts also charged their fixed guns, while their radiomen unshipped the .30-caliber Brownings aft. Both pilots climbed to 1,000 feet and set course for Ford Island, but soon noticed that smoke, boiling up from the burning planes on the mat at Ewa, obscured Pearl Harbor from view. Looking up, the two American pilots saw another 20 Japanese planes heading directly at them. Quickly deciding that they might not survive a try at landing at Ford Island, Deacon pushed the SBD into a dive, levelling off at 200 feet above the coast of Oahu with Roberts in 6-B-9 close behind. They were bound for Hickam Field, the sprawling Army bomber base on the east side of the entrance channel to Pearl Harbor.

However, west of that channel lay Fort Weaver, an Army post and site of the Fleet Machine Gun School. The appearance of two low-flying planes

Fort Weaver, near the entrance to Pearl Harbor, 19 August 1941; ENSs Deacon and Roberts skirted this U.S. Army post on the morning of 7 December as they approached Hickam Field (upper R). (38898 A.C.)

Army crash boats, marked with prominent centered stars identical to the insignia of American aircraft, lie alongside the boat dock at Hickam in late 1941. (S.C.128062)

presented the soldiers and marines (with itchy trigger fingers and tempers aroused to a fever pitch by the Japanese attack) an opportunity to try and extract a small measure of retribution.

The marine detachment at the Fleet Machine Gun School had been alerted at 0800, and had their .50-caliber Browning water-cooled machine guns and 20-milimeter Oerlikons (the latter a type of weapon the ships of the fleet were soon to receive in quantity) ready to fire by 0810, and had engaged the enemy—torpedo planes clearing Pearl Harbor or high-level bombers approaching from the south—at that moment. Alerted at 0810, perhaps by the marines' fire, the Headquarters battery of the 97th Coast Artillery had been ready to fire by 0813, opening up a minute later. Battery "G," alerted simultaneously, had its guns ready to fire by 0830.

As Deacon and his wingman roared low down the coast, weapons ranging from Browning Automatic Rifles and .30-caliber Springfield '03s, .50-caliber and .30-caliber, and 20-millimeter antiaircraft machine guns, to 3-inch antiaircraft guns, were in action and manned by soldiers or marines ready to use them. Ironically, a gunner's mate 3d class from *Enterprise* and four marines from the carrier's marine detachment were on temporary duty at the Fleet Machine Gun School, too.

Tracers flew toward the two SBDs, hitting both as they flew near the bestirred hornet's nest at Fort Weaver. Shortly after the firing started below, two "Zero" fighters commenced a shallow dive and made a firing pass on Deacon's SBD. At about the same time, Coslett noted the tracers from the guns at the Army post starting out small and growing larger until they hit home; bullets tearing into Six-Sail-Fourteen knocked the machine gun from Coslett's grasp as he sat facing aft, and inflicted serious wounds in his right wrist, right shoulder and on the right side of his neck; in the front cockpit, bullets knicked Deacon's left thigh and cut his parachute straps at the cushion. As Bill Roberts looked on, and felt "friendly" rounds strike his own plane, Deacon's SBD-3 lurched upward for a moment and then fell sharply toward the water, trailing a thin plume of smoke or gasoline; its engine then sputtered and lost power.

Headquarters building at Hickam, 24 November 1939; it was into this building that ENS Roberts ran to try and find a telephone to call Pearl Harbor and inform them of the Japanese attack. (38836 A.C.)

Struggling to control his battered plane and "damned mad" that he was being shot down by "friendly" fire, Ed Deacon made a wheels-up, full-stall landing in the shallows just short of Hickam's runway. Wounded, himself, although less seriously than his passenger, Deacon clambered stiffly from his cockpit and made his way aft to his bleeding radioman. Reaching inside the after cockpit and ripping out a radio cord, the pilot deftly fashioned a makeshift tourniquet and bound up Coslett's shattered forearm (a bullet had knocked two inches of bone from the ulna), and then broke out the life raft from its compartment on the port side of the fuselage aft of the gunner's cockpit. After helping the lanky Coslett into the rubber boat, Deacon got in and they set out for the shoreline that lay 200 yards away across water swept with rifle fire from soldiers who seemed inclined to fire first and ask questions later. Fortunately for the two men in the raft, the soldiers firing at them possessed more enthusiasm than skill as marksmen.

While Deacon was paddling for shore with his wounded radioman, covering about half the distance from the crashed plane to land (about 100 yards), an Army crash boat set out from the boat dock at Hickam. Its crew, seeing the star insignia on the aircraft, drew near and picked up the two men, put about and headed for the boat dock. More rifle fire came from the shore from the edgy soldiers, and as Ed Deacon crouched behind the gunwale of the crash boat, the thought crossed his mind that plywood couldn't stop gunfire!

Meanwhile, having lost sight of his section leader, Bill Roberts noticed gasoline streaming from his own left wing. His passenger almost bailed out, but seeing that 6-B-9 was still airborne, elected to stay on board. Neither man had suffered any injuries, although some bullets passing through the after cockpit had torn Jones' pants legs; the battery located aft on the floor of the cockpit stopped several, though, that might otherwise have hit him. Landing at Hickam, Roberts taxied the SBD near the administration build-ing, and after it had rolled to a stop, ran into the building and immediately tried to call Pearl Harbor. It seemed that all phones were dead, so he sent a teletype message to Pearl requesting that a warning be broadcast; as insurance, Roberts returned to his plane and sent out similar messages from the radio in 6-B-9. As things turned out, Hickam proved to offer little respite and refuge for the harried *Enterprise* aircrew. Shortly after 0900, 27 Nakajima B5N2s from *Zuikaku*, together with many low level strafing aircraft from *Akagi* attacked the base. "Pooky" Jones manned the single .30 caliber Browning machine gun and exhausted his ammunition firing at the strafers.

After the attack, Bill Roberts looked over his aircraft and assessed the damage: "ignition wire to the rear spark plug of number three cylinder cut, both left fuel tanks punctured, landing light broken, skin and stringers of wings torn in numerous places, engine cowling torn, left aileron and left elevator pierced." Fortunately, both Roberts and Jones made it through the morning's events unhurt, and ultimately repaired the plane themselves (with Jones installing a new ignition harness himself).

Meanwhile, Deacon and Coslett had reached shore, and the pilot helped his wounded radioman toward an aid station. On their way, they met an Army sergeant carrying a box containing what looked like several half-pint bottles of "Old Crow" whiskey. The sergeant looked at the bloodied Coslett and said: "Here, sailor, you look like you could use this," and opened a bottle for him. Gratefully downing the "Old Crow," the young radioman was feeling considerably less pain by the time he reached the aid station. Eventually reaching their destination, Deacon and Coslett—the latter with a Mercurochrome "T" painted on his forehead to signify his need for a tetanus shot—rode an ambulance to an aid station at the bomber base. Six-Sail-Fourteen failed to receive the same attention in the post-attack clean-up; she languished in the shallows for two weeks before being recovered and sent to NAS Pearl Harbor for disposition.

CHAPTER IV

. . . . .

"Refuel, Rearm, and Rejoin."

Meanwhile, back on board *Enterprise*, disbelief, shock, and then acceptance greeted the news of the Japanese attack. Breakfast had hardly settled when, at 0823, *Enterprise* had picked up an urgent message from CINCPAC: ALERT X JAPANESE PLANES ATTACKING PEARL AND AIR FIELDS ON OAHU.

Shortly thereafter, the carrier's radiomen picked up other frantic messages, including those from men in Scouting SIX and Bombing SIX in fights for their lives off Oahu. Soon, radio traffic concerning the raid on Pearl Harbor and nearby military and air facilities literally jammed the airwaves. For Scouting SIX—most of which had been on the morning search—the sudden outbreak of hostilities had drastically reduced its ability to operate from the ship. It had 18 aircraft on strength (16 operational) on 7 December. Not counting Ben Troemel's and Earl Donnell's, 13 had departed on the morning search. With 6-S-17 and 6-S-18 restored to operational status, that left five available planes. Three of the remaining eight pilots assigned to VS-6, however, were relatively new to the squadron and had not yet been carrier-qualified: ENSs Reid Stone, Daniel Seid, and Percy W. Forman (all A-V(N), USNR). That left three experienced pilots—LT(jg) Norman J. "Dusty" Kleiss, ENS J. Norman West and ENS Horace I. Proulx, A-V(N), USNR—to fly the remaining aircraft. Those three had, in fact, been scheduled to fly Scouting SIX's afternoon search on the 7th.

At 0830, *Enterprise* went to general quarters. The guttural growl of the klaxons galvanized the deck crew into action, and these men nimbly brought all operational fighters to the flight deck. Ordinarily, "flight quarters" preceded any launch, but this time the fighter pilots on standby received no warning or briefing—just the strident command, "Pilots, Man Your Planes."

Four VF-6 pilots arrived on the flight deck to find blue smoke spewing from beneath their planes as Pratt and Whitneys roared to life, an acrid haze enveloping the stubby "Wildcats." Usually, only the pilots started their own aircraft; as ENS Jim Daniels

mounted 6-F-17, his young plane captain insisted, almost apologetically, over the roar of the engines: "Mr. Daniels, they told me to start the airplane. They *told* me!" With only a short time to warm up their engines, the four pilots brought their F4F-3s into position for launch. At that instant, one of the plane handlers held up a small chalkboard with the words: JAPS ATTACK PEARL HARBOR with an expletive added to lend authenticity to the announcement. Orders soon came to launch four ready fighters and send the remainder down to the hangar deck via number one elevator to clear the flight deck. *Enterprise* launched her CAP into a stiff east-northeasterly wind at 0915, just three minutes after a message arrived in the carrier's radio room to execute War Plan 46 against Japan.

Enterprise's first wartime CAP

6-F-3	LT(jg) Frederick F. Hebel
6-F-12	LT(jg) Eric Allen
6-F-8	ENS John C. Kelley
6-F-17	ENS James G. Daniels, III

Fifteen minutes after the four F4Fs had roared into the sky, *Enterprise*'s loudspeakers declared that a state of war existed between the United States and Japan. With the deck clear of fighters, the flight deck crew spotted 15 SBDs, mostly from Bombing SIX, while arming crews trundled 1,000-pound bombs out to them, so that they could be sent aloft to seek out the foe. Lacking concrete information as to where the enemy lay, though, Halsey could do nothing except wait.

Back at Pearl Harbor, meanwhile, as various individual sections of the morning search flight were attempting to land in some fashion, Young and Nichol reached Kimmel's headquarters at the submarine base after their boat ride from Ford Island. They reported in, made their mission known, and informed those they found there that other planes were trying to get in, too. At 0908, COM 14 warned all ships present at Pearl: DO NOT FIRE ON OUR

The submarine base, Pearl Harbor, 17 October 1941, looking north. After their landing on 7 December, LCDRs Young and Nichol repaired to ADM Kimmel's headquarters on the second floor of the two-story building (R) near the submarine escape training tank. Among the ships at the piers (L) include the submarines seen by LT(jg) Jack Blitch of VB-6 on 29 November, *Narwhal* (SS-167) and *Dolphin* (SS-169). Visible at the top of this view are the battleships *Arizona* and *Nevada*, moored where they would be on the morning of the Japanese attack. (80-G-115424)

PLANES COMING IN. In the proverbial heat of battle, though, few apparently paid attention to the message.

Meanwhile, Earl Gallaher and Willy West had decided to try a landing at Ford Island shortly before 0900, but the heavy barrage of antiaircraft fire that greeted them foiled their attempt to get down. The inhospitable nature of their reception — even given the understandable edginess of the defenders under the circumstances — was due, in part, to the Japanese second wave attack just then getting underway.

Gallaher and West returned thence to Barbers Point to wait, and, circling nervously between there and Ewa, soon had company: ENS Weber, who had lost his section leader off Kaena Point almost a half hour before. Soon thereafter, another section of SBDs arrived: Dale Hilton and Bud Kroeger, who had reached Oahu at about 0900, had seen the smoke soiling the Hawaiian sky and closed in on their three circling shipmates at 0915. Kroeger saw the great quantity of smoke and switched frequencies from KGU to ship and learned of the attack.

Shortly after 0915, "Misty" Fogg and "Dobby" Dobson arrived on the scene, too, swelling the little company to seven. Fogg and Dobson had arrived over Oahu around 0837. The latter noted planes burning on the mat at Ewa and initially thought of sabotage. The marine colonel at the field undoubtedly would "have a lot of explaining to do" about the wrecked aircraft. Then Dobson saw "all the guns at [Pearl Harbor] blasting away full force." It all looked so unreal, and even after he saw those things he still could not make his "mind register that *we were in war*."

For several minutes this little flock of *Enterprise* planes circled between Ewa and Barbers Point at an altitude of 400 to 500 feet, before Gallaher noticed what looked like Japanese planes some 3,500 feet above them. Dobson's radioman, Hoss, looked up from working in the after cockpit with wide-eyed astonishment. The enemy pilots, however, either did not see the Americans or were preoccupied with other tasks, for they did not attack. Scouting SIX's XO then exhibited the leadership qualities that would stand him in good stead when the chips were down. He gathered his men for mutual protection and led them away from the south coast. Keeping his little force intact, Gallaher led

Planes burning at Ewa Mooring Mast Field, near Barbers Point, alerted incoming *Enterprise* pilots to the fact that things were far from normal on the morning of 7 December. Here, a Vought SB2U-3 "Vindicator" burns; wing fabric on the right wing has already burned off, and the plane has broken in half. (Larkin Collection, MCHC)

Three Aichi D3A1 Type 99 carrier bombers ("Val") from *Kaga* attack the battleship *Nevada*. The photograph was taken from Ford Island; LCDR "Brigham" Young witnessed the same attack from ADM Kimmel's headquarters at the Submarine Base. (80-G-32671)

Nevada passes Ford Island in her bid for the open sea. *Pennsylvania* (BB-38), immobile in Dry Dock No. 1, can be seen in the background. LT Dickinson saw *Nevada* shortly afterward at the conclusion of her magnificent failure to escape Pearl, from his vantage point across the channel. (USN)

it to a point some five to ten miles out to sea and awaited further developments.

Back at Pearl Harbor, the Japanese second wave numbered *Nevada*, the only battleship that had gotten underway during the first strike, among their targets. Twenty-one Type 99s from *Kaga* concentrated upon her as she attempted to sortie. "Brigham" Young, after making his report at Kimmel's headquarters, observed *Nevada*'s travail with a trained eye and more than detached interest. He later called the Japanese attack "practically perfect," with the Aichis making shallow 50 degree dives, out of the sun, with longer intervals between planes than was American practice. Young saw no aircraft shot down during the bombing runs, and attributed that to the determined nature of the onslaught, Japanese evasive action, and—something to which he probably owed his being alive—relatively ineffective American antiaircraft fire. Soon afterwards, Young received orders to return to Ford Island and report to RADM Patrick N. L. Bellinger, COMPATWING TWO.

Another observer to the end of *Nevada*'s gallant attempt to make the open sea was LT Dickinson, who had experienced many adventures since he had bailed out of his spinning SBD-3 near Ewa. Beneath the silk canopy of his parachute, Dickinson had drifted toward a freshly graded dirt road, hearing his plane explode as it crashed in the vicinity. Somersaulting backwards upon landing, the aviator tumbled into a bush. Regaining his wind and his feet, Dickinson untangled himself from his parachute straps and soon spied a red panel truck heading towards him. Attempts to obtain a ride proved futile. The driver looked Japanese (he was probably Nisei), and was obviously scared, for he quickly fled with his truck and left Dickinson cursing in the dust.

Driven by the dominant thought that he *had* to get to Pearl somehow, Dickinson set out, orienting himself by the smoke columns. He reached the main road after walking and running nearly a quarter-mile, and soon flagged down the blue sedan driven by Mr. Otto F. Heine, who, along with his wife, was motoring to a picnic at Fort Weaver. Initially, the Heines didn't comprehend the gravity of the situation and Dickinson's predicament until the sight of a low-flying Japanese plane convinced them that there was a war on. Slaking his thirst with a Coca-Cola commandeered for the war effort ("It's on the house," he told the Nisei operators of a roadside store), Dickinson watched with professional interest what Japanese planes he could see as his now solicitous hosts—whose car would be strafed en route to Pearl Harbor—took their hitchhiker where he needed to go.

Having had the Heines drop him off at the en-

At Ewa Mooring Mast Field, marines armed with Springfield model '03 rifles fire back at Japanese aircraft on the morning of 7 December from the site of the unfinished pool. Note SBD (upper L) and marines' headgear—garrison caps and a Hawley helmet.
(USMC via Lord)

trance to Hickam Field, Dickinson ran toward the gate of the naval reservation. Marines there were methodically firing at strafing planes with Springfield '03s when a station wagon, driven by CAPT Lloyd J. "Jerry" Wiltse, CO of the light cruiser *Detroit* (CL-8), screeched to a halt, jammed with men. One more didn't matter, and it did beat walking, so the pilot piled in and rode for a few blocks, until Wiltse reached the Officer's Club landing, after which time Dickinson secured another ride, this time with a Filipino mess steward who drove him within 20 yards of the hospital landing, from which vantage point he saw *Nevada* stopped in the south channel around 0916, her gallant sortie attempt a magnificent failure that nonetheless inspired every man who witnessed it. Inside 15 minutes, Dickinson had arrived on Ford Island, and made his way across the field to where the carrier groups normally based when not embarked on board ship. He saw only three planes that looked familiar, as well as Perry Teaff and the "skipper," Hopping, who "was as glad to see me as I was to see him." No one else from Scouting SIX

had yet made it in.

Of the 18 pilots that had taken off that morning, five had been shot down by the Japanese (Gonzalez, Willis, Dickinson, McCarthy and Vogt) and one (Deacon) by the Americans. Roberts was at Hickam Field, Patriarca was searching gamely for *Enterprise*, Gallaher had gathered six planes to his own; while Hopping, Teaff, and Young had landed at Ford Island. Roberts' transmission to *Enterprise* had provided only a glimpse of what had transpired that morning. "From best information," COMAIRBATFOR's war diary states, "some of our planes...arrived just in the midst of the Japanese attack and were shot down by their planes and by our own antiaircraft on Oahu. A terrible thought, but the hysteria undoubtedly caused by the surprise attack caused the defending forces to fire at any approaching planes without a thought as to the possible friendliness . . ."

For about 45 minutes, Gallaher's brood had waited for the situation on Oahu to settle down so they might have, at the very least, a fair chance of landing without becoming either an American or a Japanese target. They watched helplessly as the second wave of Japanese planes sowed destruction and then headed for home, the seven SBDs seemingly always sandwiched in on every quarter by enemy aircraft. About 0945, Gallaher decided to attempt a landing, choosing Ewa over Pearl, probably because of the high volume of antiaircraft fire still visible over the latter. The marines at Ewa possessed only .30-caliber machine guns taken from destroyed aircraft, water-cooled .30-caliber machine guns, and rifles—hence the relatively clear skies over the marine field.

Precisely what Gallaher's weary troops expected in the way of a reception is not known. What they received, however, could scarcely be called an enthusiastic welcome. No sooner had Gallaher and Dobson touched down when a marine sprinted up to their planes. Over the roar of the engines, they heard him shout, "For God's sake, get into the air or they'll strafe you, too!" Willy West, who landed at almost the same time, saw marines motioning for them to take off.

Dutifully, Earl Gallaher shoved his throttle forward and took off, followed by his brood. As Master Technical Sergeant Charles S. Barker, Jr., USMC, recorded in MAG-21's "Record of Events" for that day, the *Enterprise* SBDs were "told to take off and stay in the air until (the) air raid was over." While on the one hand it may have seemed better for the Navy pilots to have their planes aloft for *their* sakes, on the other the marines did not need fresh targets to draw enemy attention. Twice that morning, Japanese planes had strafed what they wanted to, seemingly impervious to ground fire and unhindered by American planes.

Gallaher, Dobson and West—the first to land at Ewa—took off immediately in right echelon and pulled up to 400 feet, with the other four close behind. An even less hospitable reception awaited them at Ford Island, as antiaircraft guns all across the harbor opened up on the newly arrived "attack wave." To "Dobby" Dobson, it seemed as if every gun on the island had begun firing almost as soon as his wheels and flaps were down. Tracers flew "thick and fast," and a shell burst just off the SBD's right wing, tipping the plane on its side. Dobson quickly grabbed the appropriate lever and dropped the seat so that the Wright-Cyclone could afford him some protection! He gave the SBD "full gun" and dove for the mat, arriving at the edge of it with what he saw was 50 knots extra speed. As the "Dauntless" seemed to float downward, Dobson at that instant had a terrible thought: "What if one of the bullets had hit a tire and blew it out?"

Afraid of "rolling the plane up in a ball" if he did have a flat tire, he felt singularly relieved when his wheels touched the surface of the landing mat and nothing happened. Pulling the tail down to complete getting his aircraft on the ground, the Oklahoman then "stomped the brakes." Six-Sail-Eight ground-looped slightly off the other end of the mat but suffered no damage, and Dobson taxied over to the hangars. The heavy but wildly inaccurate fire notwithstanding, Gallaher, Dobson and West landed safely at 0945. Only West reported damage—two or three holes in his left wing. Hav-

ing witnessed the hot reception accorded their three shipmates—and under fire themselves—Hilton, Fogg, Kroeger and Weber elected to return to Ewa. The four SBDs quickly broke away from the skies over Pearl and returned to the marine field around 1000, where the leathernecks proved more hospitable this time around, refuelling and arming the SBDs. By 1015, marines had finished arming Weber's and Kroeger's planes, and Hilton's soon thereafter.

At the same time, out at sea to the westward of Oahu, *Enterprise* was turning into the wind, and soon commenced launch of three additional fighters at 1015—Fighting SIX's XO, LT Frank T. Corbin in 6-F-11, along with ENS Herbert H. Menges, A-V(N), USNR, in 6-F-10 and ENS David R. Flynn, A-V(N), USNR, in 6-F-6—to serve as TF 8's inner air patrol. Their shipmates in Fighting SIX that had taken to the air earlier had kept an uneasy vigil, sighting nothing but whitecaps and clouds. TF 8, meanwhile, maneuvered south of Kaula Rock, "pending further information and instructions." *Enterprise* had received so many false reports from "unknown sources concerning presence of enemy ships,carriers,transports, and submarines," COMAIRBATFOR's war diarist wrote, "that it is very difficult to glean the true from the false."

Among the reports later proved false was one telling of two enemy carriers some 30 miles south of Barbers Point. Shortly after Corbin's VF-6 section took to the air, *Enterprise* commenced launching 15 SBDs at 1020, including the remaining Scouting SIX aircraft, to attack the two enemy flattops. "Dusty" Kleiss, having flown the SBD-2 type aircraft since late October, was assigned an SBD-3 (BuNo 4565) originally earmarked for Scouting TWO and still bearing the markings 2-S-18. John W. Snowden, RM3c, rode in the rear seat as radio-gunner. LT(jg) James W. McCauley, with Stuart J. Mason, Jr., RM3c as his radio-gunner, felt a variety and intensity of emotions—"dedication, determination, anxiety, apprehension and relief from tension"—as he prepared to take off from *Enterprise*'s flight deck. "What we had been anxiously expecting," he later wrote, "had come to pass . . . " As he sat in the cockpit, though, he happened to glance up at *Enterprise*'s island as the ship "ran up the largest and most beautiful American flag I'd ever seen . . ."

For a brief time, the airborne SBDs orbited *Enterprise* while Halsey and CAPT Murray and their respective staffs considered their options. One of the "carriers" spotted by jittery search plane pilots that morning soon proved to be *Minneapolis* (CA-36), the identification of which prompted a cancellation of orders to go after her.

"Dusty" Kleiss soon received orders to look for

a tanker approximately 70 miles from the ship and bearing southeast by south. Kleiss, along with Norm West and Proulx, and three VB-6 aircraft, had no sooner started to search when he heard another message in his earphones that impressed him as a "drill" message sent out by the Army. The six planes soon arrived at the spot indicated by their orders, and formed a scouting line to sweep the area completely. While searching that area, Kleiss heard a "faint, but clear" transmission: ALL PLANES FROM FORD ISLAND FIELD TOWER, USE CAUTION . . . CLIPPER IS . . . followed by static. Kleiss concluded that the whole evolution was a drill, and mentally altered the odds of it being real from 50-50 to 10-1; "Surely," he reasoned, "one of our pilots would give a position report, or give his call letters or name, or one of the messages would make sense!" Why send a group of planes, armed with bombs, on a search for a tanker that was not within miles of her reported position when *enemy carriers* were on the rampage? It did not make sense.

These sightings likewise prompted RADM Bellinger, to whom LCDR Hopping reported in the absence of LCDR Young, to direct Scouting SIX's skipper to send one plane to check out these reports of the two enemy carriers. Bellinger's orders were to search out between 25 and 40 miles, and to hold (the) remaining planes on the ground as an attack group." Although Hopping had a few men to detail to the task at hand, he apparently did not want to order someone to do something he would not do himself.

Jumpy gunners took Scouting SIX's skipper under fire at 1030, and Six-Sail-One briefly became a target for the second time that morning. From Barbers Point, Hopping flew tracks west 20 miles, south 20

miles, west 60 miles, south 20 miles, east 60 miles; during the course of the flight, he and his radioman only saw American ships and a few sampans.

On the return flight to *Enterprise*, "Dusty" Kleiss recomputed the odds against this whole thing being real from 10 to 1 to 50 to 1. However, as he circled 2-S-18 to come on board, his eyes perceived something never done in a drill: *Enterprise* was flying her battle ensign. Dick Best had seen it, too, an impressive and unforgettable sight, as he entered the landing circle. Halsey had ordered the battle flags broken out at 1105, shortly after he had radioed CINCPAC that he (Halsey) was relying on Kimmel to provide scouting information. COMAIRBATFOR possessed too few planes to track down all of the babble of sighting reports, and Halsey wanted to "maintain an effective carrier striking group in readiness" for whatever might turn up. Halsey then ordered his cruisers to conduct a search with their aircraft; *Northampton, Chester* and *Salt Lake City* each, in turn, launched two Curtiss SOCs to search sectors that lay to the north-northeast, out to 150 miles.

At 1045, meanwhile, while Hopping was carrying out his lone search, LTCOL Larkin and his staff made a quick estimate of the damage wrought by the Japanese that morning, and reported same to ADM Kimmel's headquarters. Larkin then informed the Interceptor Command center at Wheeler Field of the number of planes available at Ewa, at 1050. A return call from Wheeler directed "available

ENS Carl Fogg's SBD-2 (BuNo 2172), 6-S-11, at Ewa Mooring Mast Field around noon on 7 December 1941. Note wrecked VMF-211 F4F-3 in background (left). Bomb cart being towed by the truck (foreground, R), invented and built locally under contract by MAG-21, was known as the "MAG Bomb Trailer, Mk. I." (Larkin Collection, MCHC)

planes . . . [to] rendezvous with B17s over Hickam Field." Since Fogg's 6-S-11 had not yet been serviced and was not ready to take off, Kroeger, Weber and Hilton departed between 1112 and 1115 for Hickam, with Hilton in the lead.

Soon thereafter, the three found themselves under antiaircraft fire at 2,000 feet, west of Ford Island; Hilton then led the two Bombing SIX pilots "down low behind and north of Ford Island" to rendezvous with the Army bombers over Hickam. Upon arrival at the rendezvous, however, the Navy pilots saw neither any planes taking off nor any in the air (these had, in fact, already taken off: three Douglas A-20s followed shortly thereafter by a pair of Boeing B-17Ds). Happily, at that moment, Hilton heard his CO report that he was over Barbers Point, on the return leg of his search, and called him over the radio, telling him of his position. Hopping, who had just received orders from *Enterprise* to "refuel, rearm, and rejoin," passed that word to Hilton, and told him to take his planes to Ford Island. At 1130, they landed.

A small amount of antiaircraft fire greeted Hopping's arrival at Ford Island at 1145, and he soon reported to RADM Bellinger that "there were no Japanese surface craft within (a) rectangle covering (the) area 100 miles west and 60 miles south of Barbers Point" and informed him of the orders he had received from the ship. COMPATWING TWO then ordered Hopping to take out a group to search the sector northwest by north to northeast by north of Oahu, attacking any enemy forces encountered before returning to Ford Island.

Meanwhile, at the same moment LCDR Hopping was touching down at Ford Island, a weary Pat Patriarca was settling his SBD-3P down onto the Army Air Corps' Burns Field, the auxiliary strip on the island of Kauai. Having been unable to find *Enterprise*, and with his fuel gauge wobbling near empty, Patriarca landed at 1145. Soon thereafter, an Army doctor there, seeing the anxiety and strain of the five and a half hours spent in the cockpit evident on the pilot's face, grounded him. Reminiscing over the events of that morning, the normally jovial and happy-go-lucky "Pat" Patriarca later quipped: "I must've looked like I needed a rest." The Army, meanwhile, "drafted" Joe DeLuca into the ground-defense forces, along with his .30-caliber machine gun and his six 100-round cans of ammunition.

Yet while Patriarca was being grounded, his land-based shipmates were getting ready to take to the air. "Brigham" Young, now back at Ford Island, reported to RADM Bellinger and took stock of the planes he had available to him. Of the 18 that had taken off from *Enterprise* on the morning search, only ten were

on Ford Island (Roberts was at Hickam and Fogg still at Ewa). Bellinger ordered Young to send out nine planes to search 175 miles out, from the north-northwest to the north-northeast of Oahu, with the remaining available aircraft and investigate reports of hostile surface ships and sampans south of Barbers Point. If they found the enemy vessels, they were to bomb and strafe them.

Young obtained permission from RADM Bellinger to station himself in the land plane control tower at Ford Island, to communicate directly with both the planes from the *Enterprise* Air Group and the ship. Up to that point, only LT Erickson, USCG, had been on duty there. As assistant operations officer for NAS Pearl Harbor, the Coast Guard pilot had sprinted from the administration building to take charge of the land plane control tower shortly after 0800, as well as the machine gun battery set up on the roof of the operations building. Unfortunately, Young soon discovered that the low-power transmitter available to him did not allow him to reach either *Enterprise*'s airborne planes or the ship.

Gunner Coles having produced the bombs, nine of the Ford Island-based planes of the *Enterprise* Air Group took off under LCDR Hopping around noon. With LCDR Young in the tower, LT Dickinson—who had apparently told no one of the ordeal he had been through since the day had begun—had been assigned the CEAG's SBD-2. Answering the call for volunteers, James L. Young, Jr., AMM3c, a young sailor from VP-22, stepped forward to serve as Dickinson's radioman. Young, from Little Rock, Ark., had enlisted in the Navy in June 1940 and had joined VP-22 in March 1941.

TASK ORGANIZATION P. M. SEARCH

PLANE	PILOT/RADIO-GUNNER	SECTOR (DEGREES,TRUE)
6-S-1	LCDR Hopping/Thomas, RM1c	350-010
6-S-2	ENS Teaff/Jinks, RM3c	350-010
6-B-5	ENS Kroeger/Chapman, RM2c	350-010
6-S-10	LT Gallaher/Merritt, RM1c	010-030
6-S-5	ENS West/Hansen, RM3c	010-030
6-S-8	ENS Dobson/Hoss, RM3c	010-030
CEAG	LT Dickinson/Young, AMM3c	330-350
6-S-7	LT(jg) Hilton/Leaming, RM2c	330-350
6-B-12	ENS Weber/Keaney, SEA1c	330-350

For over three hours, those three-plane sections sought the enemy in the waters north of Oahu. As *Enterprise* and the elements of her air group were

VADM Patrick N. L. Bellinger, COMPATWING TWO (as RADM) at the time of the Japanese attack on Pearl Harbor. 1943 Photographic portrait by Maurice Constant. (NH 51529)

hunting the enemy, spirited discussions were taking place simultaneously on board the flagship of the 1st Air Fleet, the aircraft carrier *Akagi*. CDR Mitsuo Fuchida, who had led the attacking planes, argued vehemently for a second strike on Pearl Harbor. He was confident that this second go at the Pacific Fleet—attacks by dive bombers on shipping and high-level bombers on the tank farms and yard facilities—would cripple not only the fleet but its base as well. Devastate the ships and their base at Pearl, and then seek out and destroy *Enterprise* and TF 8, which they knew were operating within striking distance! Fuchida spoke for just about every pilot in the 1st Air Fleet.

VADM Chuichi Nagumo, however, did not share Fuchida's eagerness to go back. The admiral believed that the Hawaii Operation had achieved—beyond the wildest Japanese imaginings—its goal. From the reports available to him from the various air groups from the six carriers of the fleet, the United States Pacific Fleet had been dealt a severe blow. Nagumo believed that he had pushed his proverbial luck to the utmost. He ordered his ships to shape a course home. Fuchida retired to his cabin in a foul mood, and sulked there for two days.

Nagumo's decision to head for home boded well for the men now looking for him. Had Hopping found the 1st Air Fleet and attacked—without fighter cover and the planes lacking self-sealing fuel tanks and armor—it is extremely doubtful that many (if any) of the 18 men would have lived to tell the tale. Such an attack would have clearly bordered on the suicidal.

At 1545, Hopping led his men back down to Ford Island. Perhaps the most glad to be back in one piece were Perry Teaff and his radio-gunner, who had had to effect temporary repairs to 6-S-2 themselves after they had landed earlier that morning. Soon after takeoff, Teaff had noted with alarm that the oil temperature in the SBD's engine had climbed to well over the "desired" range and into the "emergency only" range. Learning of his wingman's plight, Hopping authorized Teaff to return at his own discretion. Nevertheless, the indomitable Oklahoman kept an eye on the gage and elected to continue the flight. On the return leg, the Wright Cyclone began to "miss" badly, and Teaff found it difficult to lower the landing gear. Back on the ground, pilot and radioman examined the plane again and found that one of the bullets from the fighter that had attacked them earlier that morning had lodged in the engine, and others had damaged the hydraulic system. A trip to the repair shop at Ford Island awaited BuNo 2175. Teaff's courage and disregard for his own safety in continuing the search, when little chance for rescue existed, earned him the Navy Cross.

While Hopping's group had been out searching, *Enterprise* had maintained the inner and combat air patrols in the vicinity of TF 8. She commenced sending aloft a CAP under Fighting SIX's CO, LCDR C. Wade McClusky, at 1230, consisting of McClusky (in 6-F-1), LT(jg) Rawie (6-F-4), ENS Gayle L. Hermann (6-F-5) and ENS Thomas C. Provost, A-V(N), USNR (6-F-15). Fuel on board all ships, meanwhile, was low: *Enterprise* had 50% on hand, but the cruisers possessed 30% and the destroyers only 20%.

Having recovered the 15 SBDs that had been aloft since around 1020 on the unsuccessful search for the enemy carriers off Barbers Point, and perhaps still unsatisfied about the lack of concrete sightings, Halsey ordered another search launched. At 1345, *Enterprise* turned into the wind and began launching nine SBDs for single-plane searches covering the sectors that lay to the east-southeast to southsouthwest, out to 175 miles.

Shortly after the SBDs deployed, Halsey received a dispatch from RADM Draemel, who had assembled a task force (TF 1), consisting of *Minneapolis* (CA-36), *St. Louis* (CL-49), *Phoenix* (CL-46) and *Detroit*, and 17 destroyers. COMAIRBATFOR immediately ordered TF 8 to alter course to "increase speed and expedite joining."

In the meantime, LT(jg) Jim Gray led a relief CAP division aloft at 1505, consisting of himself (in 6-F-13), ENS Kelley (6-F-8), LT(jg) Rhonald J. Hoyle (6-F-16), ENS Walter J. Hiebert, A-V(N), USNR (6-F-6), LT(jg) Roger W. Mehle (6-F-3), and ENS Harold N.

Heisel (6-F-17). LCDR McClusky brought his division on board 15 minutes later.

Had Japanese carriers been operating off Oahu as the welter of reports indicated, Halsey suspected that they would retire homeward via Jaluit, in the Mandated Islands. At 1552, COMAIRBATFOR ordered TF 12, having called off the mission to ferry VMSB-231 to Midway, to intercept and destroy the Japanese if the enemy happened to be moving that direction. Soon thereafter, however, the beleaguered TF 8 would have to try and find yet another phantom flattop.

LT(jg) Clifford R. Walters (*circa* March 1942). (USN)

CHAPTER V

· · · · ·

"My God, What's Happened?"

he SOCs launched from Halsey's cruisers during the forenoon watch searched their respective sectors. While *Chester*'s and *Salt Lake City*'s pilots and radio-gunners found little except three sampans and a PBY, respectively, *Northampton*'s two-plane section encountered a "Zero" from *Kaga*. In the 15-minute combat, the scrappy SOCs' radio-gunners drove off the fighter and sent it away smoking. *Northampton*'s SOCs reached Pearl Harbor first (1527), followed by *Chester*'s and *Salt Lake City*'s. None had, however, sighted any Japanese ships.

During the course of his search south of Oahu, ENS Clifford R. Walters, A-V(N), USNR, though, in 6-B-17, saw what looked to him like a *Soryu*-class carrier at 1630. He circled wide to gain a position up-sun to identify the ship, but saw an aircraft—it looked like a silver, twin-engined monoplane with twin stabilizers—approaching him from his starboard quarter. He dove at full throttle, outdistancing his adversary; shortly afterward, he sighted what he identified as a "*Jintsu*-class" light cruiser (it may have been an American "flush-deck" destroyer) and, using one of the many rain squalls in the area as cover, tracked it through the reduced visibility. He reported his find, and that he was being chased by enemy fighters.

Exactly what Walters saw is a mystery. During his subsequent appearance before the Roberts Commission investigating the Pearl Harbor attack, VADM Halsey testified that he questioned the young ensign when he returned to *Enterprise* on 8 December. Halsey said that he very much doubted that Walters saw a carrier or cruiser, and then speculated that the aircraft menacing Walters that morning were Army A-20s patrolling south of Oahu. The eight A-20As which survived the Japanese onslaught on Hickam Field, however, sported neither twin-tails nor silver finishes. Moreover, the 18th Bombardment Wing A-20s had orders to search for Japanese carriers *north* of Oahu. It is more likely that Walters spotted one of two PBY-5s from VP-24 (24-P-1 or 24-P-4) that had been dispatched to look for the

elusive enemy.

Regardless of *what* he had sighted, Walters' report prompted action. Kleiss, Proulx and West, the three remaining VS-6 pilots on board (Troemel and Donnell were on searches) received instructions on laying smoke. Out on the flight deck, armorers had exchanged the bombs with which the SBDs had been equipped for 850-pound smoke tanks. With chart boards and gear, Kleiss and his two shipmates from VS-6 mounted their aircraft, expecting just to taxi them forward. To their surprise, however, they were given the signal to launch, with "no point option or ship's position or enemy position or wind data."

They joined three Bombing SIX planes, one of which was flown by LT Dick Best and another by LT(jg) Jim McCauley, to accompany 19 torpedo-armed TBD-ls from Torpedo SIX; six fighters from Fighting SIX, led by LT(jg) "Fritz" Hebel, VF-6's gunnery officer, would fly cover. Leading the strike was LT Eugene E. Lindsey, the 36-year-old skipper of Torpedo SIX. At 1642, *Enterprise* turned into the wind and commenced launch of the 31 planes into the gathering darkness.

The six fighter pilots protecting the strike group represented, like the pilots and passengers of the SBDs that had first encountered the enemy earlier that day, a cross-section of America.

Plane	Pilot
6-F-1 (BuNo 3906)	LT(jg) Francis F. Hebel
6-F-15 (BuNo 3935)	ENS Herbert H. Menges, A-V(N), USNR
6-F-5 (BuNo 3916)	ENS James G. Daniels, III
6-F-12 (BuNo 3938)	LT(jg) Eric Allen, Jr.
3-F-15 (BuNo 3982)	ENS Gayle Hermann, A-V(N), USNR
6-F-4 (BuNo 3909)	ENS David R. Flynn, A-V(N), USNR

AVCDT Francis F. "Fritz" Hebel, USNR, 8 January 1936. (NH 96618)

AVCDT Herbert H. Menges, USNR, 15 December 1939. (NH 96616)

ENS David R. Flynn, *circa* 29 January 1942. (80-G-464482, cropped)

ENS Eric "Ethan" Allen, Jr., 12 August 1940, the day after he reported to NAS Pensacola to commence flight training. (NH 96617)

LT(jg) (then-ENS) Gayle L. Hermann, *circa* 29 January 1942. (80-G-464482, cropped)

LT(jg) (then-ENS) James G. Daniels, *circa* 29 January 1942. (80-G-464482, cropped)

The leader, LT(jg) "Fritz" Hebel, hailed from Wisconsin. After graduating from California Tech with a B.S. degree, he enlisted in the Navy in 1936 to take part in the AVCTD program, and won his wings on 25 February 1937. Although he had expressed a preference for flying fighters, or bombers, from *Yorktown* (CV-5), some time would elapse before that ship was commissioned, and he was assigned instead to VO-2B (later reclassified as VO-1B), and flew Curtiss SOCs in the aviation unit of *Nevada*. Commissioned ensign A-V(N), USNR, in 1939, Hebel served for a time as flight instructor at Grosse Isle, Michigan, before he ultimately reported to VF-6 in March 1941.

Hebel's wingman, ENS Herb Menges, hailed from Louisville, Kentucky, and had attended the university there from 1935 to 1939. Enlisting in the USNR in the summer of 1939, Menges immediately reported to the Naval Reserve Aviation Base, Robertson, Missouri, for elimination flight training. Winning his wings a year and one week later, at NAS Pensacola, Menges donned his ensign's stripes on 6 September 1940. He reported on board VF-6 on 28 November of the same year.

Leading the second section was ENS Daniels, VF-6's personnel officer. The son of a Missouri state senator, Daniels had attended the University of Kansas and then the University of Southern California before a lack of finances (a common problem with college students then as now) compelled him to enlist in the USNR in April 1938. Winning his wings in August 1939, Daniels was commissioned ensign the following month, and joined Fighting SIX in October 1939.

Daniels' wingman was the only "Academy" man in the flight—LT(jg) Eric Allen, Jr., USNA Class of 1938. Nicknamed "Ethan" by his classmates, and born in Massachusetts on 22 July 1916, a minister's son, Allen had first served in the light cruiser *Trenton* (CL-11) before undergoing flight training at Pensacola. His preference for duty upon graduation had been a scouting squadron on board *Enterprise*, but after winning his wings, he was assigned to VF-6, and joined the squadron on 1 April 1941. A slender, easygoing young man with a ruddy complexion and "an infectious grin and irrepressible sense of humor," he possessed a beautiful tenor voice, and had been a crackerjack water polo player at the Academy.

Another Yankee in the flight, ENS Hermann, led the third section. A Duke University graduate, the 26-year-old New Britain, Connecticut, native had won his wings on 6 July 1939, and reported to VF-6 (his preference had been "fighters—west coast" upon graduation from Pensacola) in August. His wingman, ENS Flynn, a Cornell University graduate, had

been a manufacturing supervisor in Niagara Falls, NY. Enlisting on 15 October 1939, a little over a month and a half after war broke out in Europe, Flynn won his wings the following summer. Commissioned ensign on 10 August 1940, he had first served in Fighting THREE, before he joined VF-6 in December 1940. On 7 December 1941, he was celebrating his 27th birthday.

Draemel's TF 1, meanwhile, had just joined up with TF 8 shortly after *Enterprise* had launched planes. At 1651, from the carrier's bridge a signal lamp blinked a message to the new arrivals: ENEMY SURFACE CRAFT REPORTED AT 1630 LAT 20-32 LONG 158-16 COURSE 270 X PROCEED WITH ALL CRUISERS AND DDS LESS ENTERPRISE SCREEN ATTACK IMMEDIATELY.

While *McCall* and *Craven* remained with *Enterprise*, the rest of TF 8 joined RADM Draemel, who deployed his surface ships, knowing how little daylight remained. The first attack unit comprised the four cruisers that had sortied from Pearl, supported by nine destroyers; the scouting line comprised the remaining eight destroyers. RADM Spruance's three cruisers, meanwhile, supported by seven destroyers, made up the second attack group. The first attack unit took its station 12 miles to the westward of the scouting line, while the second attack unit steamed to the northward of the first. The plan had to be kept simple—many of the destroyers had sortied from the smoke and confusion of Pearl with only junior officers in command. The fast minelayer *Gamble* (DM-15) augmented the carrier's screen at 1736, joining *Craven* and *McCall*.

That afternoon, Jim Gray's group had maintained the CAP, but had intermittently found itself the target of Draemel's jittery gunners in TF 1 as that force and TF 8 had neared each other, between 1600 and 1715—an understandable occurrence given what the men in those ships had been through that morning. As VF-6's diarist recounted later: "Maintained Combat Air Patrol over ship 'til sunset . . . fired at on by own fleet antiaircraft. Gray seems indignant about it. Roger Mehle reported a whole fleet of ships coming, and scared us all; but it was our own . . ." *Enterprise* brought Gray and his five shipmates on board at 1740.

Flying over the water at 300-foot altitude, meanwhile, the SBDs of the attack group did gentle S-turns above the lumbering TBDs to avoid overrunning them. "Dusty" Kleiss's new aircraft was proving a frustrating mount: the cockpit lights would not work "and even if they had, my data was insufficient to navigate." Halfway to the target, a cold wave of fear washed over Jim McCauley, when he realized the full implications of the mission he was on. "We . . .would lay

View from Ford Island showing *Arizona* burning on the afternoon of 7 December. Some of the pilots who flew into Pearl from *Enterprise* later walked down to get a closer look, but were told by sentries to stay clear. (80-G-32551)

smoke for the torpedo planes. We would fly parallel to the enemy force a thousand yards out. We were on a suicide mission . . ." As Dick Best so succinctly put it, their job was to allow VT-6 "to launch their attacks with some hope of reaching the drop point without being shot out of the sky . . ." Jim McCauley fought the fear and panic that could have endangered not only himself but other pilots and radiomen in the blackness. As he later recounted, when he took off at dusk on 7 December, "I couldn't actually spit cotton." Nerves were on edge throughout the formation as it groped through the murk, seeking the enemy.

Back at Pearl, several of the intrepid band of pilots that had made the morning flight settled in for a fitful night at the old BOQ on Ford Island. Space was hard to come by, as they found that much of the building had been transformed into a hospital and nursery—virtually all of the children on Ford Island had been corralled on the second floor. Early in the evening some of the *Enterprise* men walked over to the shore near *Arizona*, which was still burning. Guards there cautioned them to "stay at a safe distance," fearing another magazine explosion.

Chow was another matter. "Dobby" Dobson and his friends managed to find some steaks in the BOQ icebox, and, lacking skillets, cooked them right on top of a range. Even eaten without salt, the meat

provided much-needed nourishment. Sleep would not come easily, though, owing to the tension-charged atmosphere on Oahu that night.

Just after nightfall, the six fighters detailed to escort the strike group had become separated from it. Hebel broke radio silence and asked the ship to transmit "yoke easy" (YE), the homing signal. What Jim Daniels later called a "beautiful piece of navigation" then brought the six fighters "right back over the ship" but *Enterprise*, apparently skittish about having to turn on lights for a night recovery in waters potentially infested with Japanese submarines, directed the six to fly to Ford Island. Not finding the "carrier" they sought, meanwhile, *Enterprise*'s attack group—*sans* escort—started back in the night that Gene Lindsey described as "as dark as the inside of a goat's belly . . ." As "Dusty" Kleiss later recorded in his diary: "The group attempted to return to (the) ship at altitude 300' speed 70 knots. With . . . smoke tanks this was most difficult for the SBDs. With no lights, no position, and only a knot or two over stalling speed at 300' we were in great danger of losing at least half the group." Jim McCauley navigated by keeping an eye on the blue exhaust flares that dotted the stygian darkness. The SBDs had had to fly with their flaps partially lowered to keep pace with the much slower TBDs.

". . . After many near collisions [and] losing sight of the formation several times," the strike group managed to reach the ship, very little fuel left in their tanks.

Enterprise, however, did not want to recover the bombers, scouts, or torpedo planes, either, and directed them to fly into Ford Island, too. Gene Lindsey, however, justifiably apprehensive over fuel consumption and the ability of the torpedo-laden TBD-1s to make it over the mountain range that ran down the spine of Oahu, pressed to come on board. *Enterprise* relented and brought the strike group home, turning on what lights she deemed sufficient for nocturnal flight operations from 2010 to 2135; an additional destroyer joined the screen shortly thereafter, when *Hull* (DD-350) arrived to take up station protecting the carrier. During the recovery operations, at about 2015, Halsey ordered Draemel to rendezvous with him at 0700 the following morning south of Oahu.

"When VT-6 got back from their fruitless search for that Jap carrier," Fighting SIX's diarist later recounted, "it was pitch dark and several of their pilots had never been up in a TBD before at night—much less with a torpedo aboard! As the torpedoes were few and precious it was decided to land them aboard, torpedoes and all, dark as it was. They all got down and no trouble." Outside of 6-T-13 fouling number one barrier at 2038, Torpedo SIX came

on board without incident. "Nice going, VT-6!" declared the VF-6 scribe, who also praised the landing signal officer, LT(jg) H. B. "Bert" Harden: "Good signaling, Harden." It was the first time in anyone's memory that torpedo planes had landed on board a carrier with live torpedoes! Harden brought the last plane in at 2113.

Dick Best breathed a relieved sigh upon landing after 4.3 hours in the cockpit; it had been the "hairiest" flight he had ever made. "When I came aboard on the night of 7 December," Best later recalled, "I had been experiencing the scariest flight of my career. My nerves were on edge from some near misses in a darkened 25-plane formation. I made the worst . . . of my 330 carrier landings. I picked up number seven wire, the next to last before the barriers, and then only because I dived for it. In the ready room, we were all exhausted and wondering what the hell was going on. On that flight I became convinced that war had started because no sane man would order flying in those conditions." Jim McCauley, who called it "one of the most rugged hops" he'd ever been on, so overcome with joy upon making it back to the ship (and with eight gallons of gas in his tanks), "got down and kissed the deck." As McCauley later recounted: "After getting back aboard . . . we were all pretty tired after a complete day of flying, so we turned in and got as much sleep as we could and stood by for the

A Douglas TBD-1 "in the groove," 29 July 1941. On the night of 7 December, the fact that these planes were landing with live torpedoes provided zest to the usual recovery operations. (80-G-21055-B)

The battleship *Pennsylvania* in dry dock no. 1 at the Pearl Harbor Navy Yard, late on 7 December; she would be there that night when her guns opened fire on LT(jg) Hebel's flight of six VF-6 "Wildcats." Note her dark gray (Measure 1) camouflage, with light gray spotting top, and CXAM-1 search radar. (80-G-32511, cropped)

Machine gun emplacements such as these along the ramp on the south end of Ford Island proliferated in the wake of the Japanese attack on 7 December. Curtiss SOCs from cruiser-based VCS units are in the background, along with a pair of PBYs, one of which (visible behind the hangar at right) has its engines warming up. *Nevada*, beached off Waipio Point, is in the background (L), visible beyond the three SOC's. (80-G-324-92)

next day."

After a half hour's flying time, meanwhile, the six F4Fs came in over Barbers Point, but in the murk, and with everything blacked out below, they went on to the next island, thinking that they had made landfall at Kauai. Definitely identifying the next island as Molokai, however, Hebel realized they had erred. He opened up on the radio and asked each pilot for his fuel status. Finding that each had enough to get him back to Oahu, Hebel turned the formation around. They made landfall in the vicinity of Koko Head at 2045, and followed the coastline around Diamond Head, past Honolulu, and east toward Hickam Field. The red and green wingtip lights glowed softly in the cool, dank night air.

As Flynn later speculated, Hebel perhaps intended to take his flight onto the lighted runway at Hickam. He then noticed lights on Ford Island—open for business and expecting their arrival—and led his men past Hickam in right echelon. Only a few minutes more and they would be on the ground.

"Brigham" Young awaited their arrival anxiously, the low-powered transmitter not having proved effective in establishing contact with his airborne planes. RADM Bellinger, too, had been concerned over the arrival of the six F4Fs. He had—several times—warned all of the ships in the harbor, and, as an added precaution, Army antiaircraft units in the area, that planes from *Enterprise* were coming in and were not to be fired upon. The planes, at least one reported version of the warning stated, would be showing green lights.

In the blackness, Hebel contacted the land plane control tower at Ford Island, and "Brigham" Young provided instructions "to come on over the field and break for landing." Hebel transmitted his intention to circle left around Ford Island. "NO," the anxious controller responded: "Come right in and land!" Hebel, however, apparently did not hear the weak signal that had proved vexing for Young ever since he had taken up his station in the tower. The six F4Fs continued circling at about 500 feet. As Hebel's flight came in from the direction of Honolulu, those below saw only green lights. As the F4Fs turned, however, the red (port) lights came into view.

CAPT Shoemaker, having returned to Quarters "A" after sunset to shed his tropical uniform and shift into warmer clothes, was driving back to the main part of the NAS when "all hell broke loose." At the sight of low-flying planes, "countless machine guns firing thousands of tracer bullets back and forth across the field" shattered the tense evening. As Theodore C. Mason, a survivor of the battered battleship *California* (BB-44) recalled: ". . . Within seconds, Pearl Harbor had erupted in a chain reac-

tion of antiaircraft fire of all calibers. The red lines of tracers formed transient geometric patterns across the sky. . . . We saw dim red and green lights approaching the airstrip from the seaward end. Most of the tracers were flashing in that direction. We took aim at the lights and opened fire with the fierce kind of joy that had possessed those brawling sailors at The Breakers in Seattle. . . . We were striking back at the foe who had so humiliated us . . ."

In bitter irony, one stray .50-caliber bullet killed Pallas F. Brown, SEA2c, a survivor from the sunken *Utah*, and wounded Leonard A. Price, SEA1c, another *Utah* survivor, on board the Base Force flagship *Argonne* (AG-31) on the east side of Ten-Ten Dock. To the Scouting and Bombing SIX pilots in the BOQ at Ford Island, it sounded like the "Japs" had come back again! Close offshore, the Japanese submarine *I-69*, on patrol south of Oahu, saw antiaircraft fire criss-crossing the sky.

As Jim Daniels later recounted in his diary: "We made the turn toward the mountains over [the] dry dock channel and all hell broke loose. The sky was ablaze with .30, .50, and 1.1 gun tracers." Daniels dove toward the lights at the southwest edge of the field, cranked up his landing gear and "went like a bat out of hell for the ocean," while hearing Fritz Hebel open up in astonishment: "My God, what's happened?"

It is difficult to determine who fired the first shot upon seeing the red lights, unleashing a veritable hail of metal hurled up at Hebel's flight, but it may have been the battleship *Pennsylvania* (BB-38) in dry dock number one. Many other ships joined in until word circulated the planes were friendly; some, though, having heard the "word," but seeing the firing commence, withheld fire anyway.

To the six stunned *Enterprise* pilots, though, the question was irrelevant. With their wheels down at low speed and altitude, they were snared in a position that made it almost impossible to evade the tracers that streaked the night.

The antiaircraft fire probably hit ENS Menges' 6-F-15 first. His plane arched in a northerly direction, across Ford Island before slanting downward and crashing into the veranda of "Palm Lodge," on Kirkbride Avenue, near the east waterfront of the Pearl City peninsula. The resulting conflagration burned the house to the ground, scorched nearby buildings, and took nearly an hour to bring under control. In the confused aftermath of the attack, authorities did not recover Menges' shattered and charred body until 11 December. ENS Dave Flynn made the positive identification three days later, when he recognized his friend's wristwatch.

Deciding to quit Pearl Harbor, Fritz Hebel headed

The auxiliary *Argonne* (AG-31), at her berth on the east side of Ten-Ten Dock on the afternoon of 7 December 1941, where she would be that night when "all hell broke loose" upon the arrival of six of Fighting SIX's F4Fs. *Oglala* (CM-4) lies capsized in the foreground. (NH 83066)

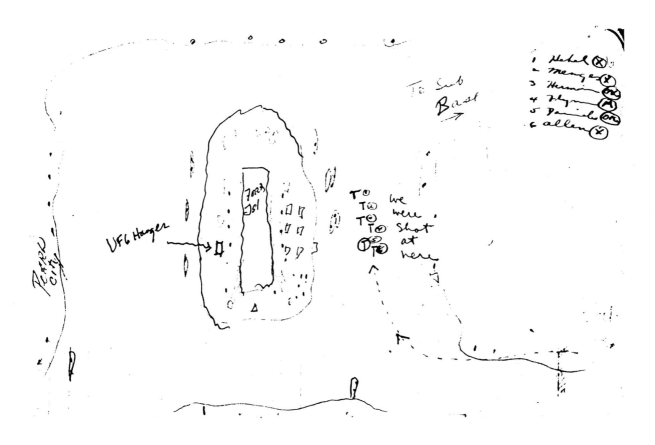

Jim Daniels' sketch of the route the six planes from VF-6 were taking when they were fired upon. (Daniels Diary, via Lundstrom)

up the valley north of Pearl toward Wheeler Field. Supposing him to be Japanese, however, Army gunners in the area fired on the F4F-3A in full deflection and shot him down. Hebel, unable to control the aircraft, tried to set down easily, but hit the ground at a flat angle glide, finally coming to rest in a gulch 200 yards west of Kunia Road, just outside Wheeler Field. Since the F4F was not equipped with shoulder straps, only lap belts, the impact thrust Hebel forward, and he suffered a severely fractured skull when his head hit the gunsight. A detail of soldiers rushed to the scene and pulled the pilot, barely alive, from the wreckage of 6-F-1. Admitted to the U.S. Army's Tripler General Hospital, Hebel died shortly thereafter, and was interred at Schofield Barracks.

After a five-inch shell passed through his F4F's engine, Gayle Hermann decided to head for NAS Ford Island. Without power, he glided his "Wildcat" down in a shower of bullets, the fire continuing even after he landed on Ford Island's little golf course. Although his plane had been holed 18 times, the pilot had miraculously escaped injury. Conscientiously gathering up his parachute, Hermann began the long trek in the dark to the hangars on the northwest side of the island.

Dave Flynn had a harrowing time of it as well. After dousing his lights, he raced ten miles out to sea from the direction of Ewa Mooring Mast Field. He turned west towards Barbers Point and then veered back toward Ewa when suddenly his F4F's Pratt and Whitney—damaged or out of fuel—sputtered and died. Flynn immediately abandoned the aircraft at 1,200 feet. The "Wildcat," meanwhile, plunged to the ground and exploded about one mile north of Barbers Point. Flynn drifted down in the darkness in the parachute he had borrowed from "Swede" Rawie earlier that day, and landed in a cane field some 2,000 yards in from the beach and four miles from Ewa, wrenching his back in the process.

Flynn's nocturnal arrival from the heavens did not go unnoticed. Soldiers of the 35th Infantry, nearby, spotted the billowing 'chute and rushed to the scene, determined to snare a Japanese parachutist. The soldiers continued rushing Flynn until some well-chosen profanity rendered "in good old United States English," with words no Japanese would probably know convinced all concerned of his friendly character. Placated, the infantrymen helped the injured ensign into an ambulance headed for Tripler. Other casualties on board were the crew of a Vought OS2U-3 "Kingfisher" from the battleship *Maryland* (BB-46) that had crashed in the dark about eight miles west of Barbers Point—LT(jg) James B. Ginn

and William R. Roberts, RM2c. Despite cuts and bruises, and head wounds that would later require 15 stitches to close, Roberts had struggled ashore with the unconscious Ginn after the crash. Although the pilot died later, Roberts would be awarded the Navy Cross for his "extraordinary heroism, courage, initiative, and disregard of his own life."

Jim Daniels, meanwhile, the last VF-6 pilot still aloft, waited for the tumult to die down before trying again. Knowing he was nearly out of gas, Daniels contacted the land plane tower, to be greeted by a voice that sounded like that of "Brigham" Young (it *was*), who initiated a curious cat-and-mouse game, that mirrored the confused paranoia of the time, by asking: "Who are you?"

"Six-Fox-Five," the pilot responded.

"What is your *name*," Young came back.

"Who are *you*," Daniels asked, wanting to make sure the individual to whom he was speaking was not Japanese. After Young had told him, and repeated his "Who are you," the pilot, reasoning that no Japanese would know the answer to the question he was about to ask, said: "I am your godchild's father—what's my middle name?"

"Ganson," Young shot back, following that up with his asking Daniels to give him *his* nickname—"Brig." The bonds of trust had been established not a minute too soon, for Daniels was very nearly out of gas!

Each having established the identity of the other, Young told the Daniels to "come in as low as possible, as fast as possible and with no lights." Daniels cranked down his gear and made his approach exactly as directed. Normally, the F4F's spring-loaded flaps dropped when the airspeed hit 130 knots. Going between 150 and 180 during the final leg of the flight, Daniels would not have the benefit of flaps for *that* landing: roaring past the foremast of the beached *Nevada*, Daniels executed an "S" turn and bore down on Ford Island's runway. Some gunfire erupted again, as it had when Fritz Hebel had led the flight in a short time before; the tracers, however, fortunately went overhead, and Daniels came in under them. Avoiding tar barrels and trucks parked to deter enemy landings, he ground-looped when he went off the ramp. Daniels fortunately did not drag a wingtip, though, and taxied back up the squadron's regular hangar, where a marine in a sandbagged gun emplacement began firing at him.

Gayle Hermann, who had meanwhile arrived in the hangar area, purportedly had to persuade the marine to stop firing with a gun butt. That unorthodox method of persuasion to "cease fire" seemed to do the trick. Hermann jumped up on Daniels' wing: "My God, Jim, you're alive!" Equally elated

The minesweeper *Vireo* (AM-52) (R) lies moored to *California*'s starboard quarter on the morning of 8 December 1941, where she lay the night before when she rescued LT(jg) Eric Allen from the oily water. Sister ship *Bobolink* (AM-20) is at left. (NH 95569)

to see his shipmate, Daniels blurted out, "Gayle, what's happened?" The spontaneous outburst of emotion reflected how the two men had been driven to their limits.

Daniels' wingman, "Ethan" Allen, did not fare as well. Struck by antiaircraft fire, Allen's "Wildcat" caught fire and exploded, giving him barely enough time to bail out of his crippled F4F over the dry dock channel. Hit by a rifle-caliber bullet on his descent, however—perhaps by jittery sailors or marines shooting at imagined Japanese paratroops—he very nearly landed on board the minesweeper *Vireo* (AM-52), which had just moored to *California*'s starboard quarter at 2100 to help in the struggle to keep that battleship afloat, coming down just astern of her and blown that direction by the prevailing winds. At that point, recalls then-PhM1c J. Lamont Norwood, *Vireo*'s pharmacist's mate, "everyone thought we had one of the Japanese." It was only after *Vireo*'s sailors pulled Allen, who had suffered bruises and internal injuries from his low-altitude bail-out, from the oily water, that they discovered "it was one of ours." Identifying Allen as an *Enterprise* pilot, *Vireo* immediately transmitted a message "to assure control" that the planes in the air were from *Enterprise*. Seeing that he was badly hurt, a *Vireo* officer then immediately ordered the wounded pilot transported so that he could receive the attention of a doctor. Apparently in great pain, he was transferred to *California* and thence to the dispensary on Ford Island, where LCDR Cecil

D. Riggs, (MC), USN, treated him. Unfortunately, there was little anyone could do at that point, but Allen clung tenaciously to life until 0200 on 8 December.

Such was the atmosphere of hysteria that the Honolulu *Star-Bulletin* the next day reported an air raid the previous evening; assistant fire chief CAPT Joseph Naone, at Hickam Field, said that the planes flew "very low with running lights on." On the night of the 7th, police—who held orders to *shoot* out any lights if necessary—had dealt with a rash of reports telling of signal lights and flares burning throughout Honolulu. Watchers reported "blinking signal lights" from West Loch and Red Hill districts, from atop the Theodore H. Davies building, and a Buddhist temple on Vineyard Street. During the raid, dispatchers ordered police cars to stop, pull off the road and darken. Furthermore, the *Star-Bulletin* related, "All cars were ordered to keep their lights off and at 11:56 police issued a warning to defense workers on the Pearl Harbor highway to stay where they were." The military police, the paper warned, had orders to "shoot on sight any cars proceeding without lights."

In one of the SBDs launched that afternoon, ENS Walters, meanwhile, whose contact report had precipitated the search that evening, found himself unable to locate the ship. He proceeded to Kaena Point, via Kauai, and, after sunset, received permission to land at Kaneohe. Earlier that day, Japanese planes had worked over the air station there pretty thoroughly—destroying 33 planes on the ramps, in the water, or in a direct hit on hangar number one—and the base had taken heavy casualties. To prevent gliders or parachutists from landing, automobiles and trucks lay parked on the mat at irregular intervals. Kaneohe, which had "a few navigational lights" on to guide returning aircraft in (a blackout had been put into effect at sundown) had been notified ahead of time that *Enterprise* planes would be coming in, but, apparently, time had not allowed them to clear the vehicles off the ramp.

Walters saw things on the ramp, dimly, but had no idea what they were. He landed in between two automobiles before he saw another in his landing lights and pulled back on the stick to jump over

it, then ground-looped and taxied up the line, weaving drunkenly between the other parked vehicles, coming to a stop with, as Walters later put it, "a damn cement mixer almost in my lap." Almost miraculously, he had made a safe landing "without denting a thing."

About a half hour after "Bucky" Walters' feat, Ben Troemel, whose day had begun with his aircraft being pushed aside for the morning flight because of the bad spark plug, neared Kaneohe, too. After 5.1 hours of flying, confronted with a pitch black night and occasional showers, the 26-year-old Troemel and his radio-gunner, Alfred R. Stitzelberger, RM3c, were glad to land. Although the blackout added to the difficulty, Troemel knew it had to be done, as he was almost out of gas. He later called his Kaneohe landing, dodging parked vehicles in the dark, "just about the most stressful maneuver I've made in my life . . ."

NAS Kaneohe, as seen from the air on 8 December 1941, the damage caused by the Japanese attack of the previous day quite apparent. (USN)

As opposed to the reception accorded the VF-6 flight at Pearl, no wild gunfire greeted Walters and Troemel as they wound up their single-plane searches at Kaneohe. "A chief petty officer who 'greeted' me after landing," Troemel recounted later, "said that Walters and I were very lucky, because we would have been shot down if there had been anything left to shoot with . . ." NAS Kaneohe's historian recounted subsequently: "The landing mat was blocked by parked automobiles . . . but [such measures] could not have been very effective because two of the *Enterprise* planes succeeded in getting down safely." Came the dawn, Walters marveled: "If it had been light when we came in, we couldn't have done it!"

At Ewa, "Misty" Fogg and Otis Lee Dennis spent a fitful night among the marines, Fogg standing ready to fly at a moment's notice. He later regaled his shipmates with stories, in his inimitable "down-east" accent, of the confusion that reigned that night, first being told to arm his plane with one weight of bomb, and then another, and so on and so forth throughout the night. His SBD represented the sole striking power available at Ewa Field.

On Kauai, Joe DeLuca, accompanied by the Army private who had been assigned to him to carry his ammunition, settled down in the dark alongside a road to be ready to repel any landing attempt. "I didn't sleep at all that night," DeLuca recounted later, "There was a lot of confusion and persons firing at imagined enemy landings . . ."

Jim Daniels and Gayle Hermann, meanwhile, had reported to Young in the land plane control tower. The day's work done, the veteran pilot took them to unoccupied quarters on Ford Island. "I think I know where the guy kept his liquor," *Enterprise's* Air Group Commander reflected once they got there, and proceeded to find it. "I think you both need a shot of whiskey."

Later, in the blacked-out quarters, Daniels noticed a telephone on the bedside table. He asked Young if he could call his wife Helen and let her know that he was all right. "Impossible," Young replied, "all the phones are out. Only official lines are open." Daniels looked at the phone, but then decided he would give it a try anyway. Dialing 98114, he was pleasantly surprised when his wife Helen answered. He told her that *Enterprise* had not been sunk as had been reported, and that he was returning to the ship in the morning. Her voice was music to his ears.

Draemel's force, meanwhile, groped through the night in search of the Japanese, but found nothing. Halsey ordered the search operations abandoned an hour before midnight on the 7th. While it had the 24 hours normally contained therein, to the men of the *Enterprise* Air Group, scattered as they were from Ewa to Tripler and from Ford Island to the ship and to Kauai, it seemed like December 7th had been an unusually long day. No one had any idea what the next would bring.

CHAPTER VI

· · · · ·

"The Highest Traditions of the Navy"

Enterprise and her four plane guards steamed to the southwest of Oahu for the rest of the night, and rendezvoused with TF 1 at daylight on the 8th for search and patrol operations. The cruisers and destroyers that had accompanied the carrier to Wake, at that point critically short of fuel, were ordered into Pearl, to arrive at 1100 on the 8th. During the night, *Enterprise*'s radar had detected the movement of those ships, and the carrier and her consorts altered course to avoid contact.

At Ford Island, Earl Gallaher saw Jack Leaming on the flight line. "Well, Leaming, are you shipping over?" "What a hell of a birthday present I received," Leaming later wrote. "I was angry, scared, and wanted to get in there and fight and get it over with and go home . . ." His sentiments echoed that of many other men. He "shipped over."

Dick Best flew in ahead of the ship with COM-AIRBATFOR's chief of staff, CDR Browning, in the back seat, so that Browning could personally obtain orders for Halsey from Kimmel himself; Best then returned to the ship with Bill Roberts as his passenger.

"Dusty" Kleiss flew a scouting hop in the morning, and through an error in sector data, ended up at one point searching the same sector as Earl Donnell. Each, oddly enough, flew plane number 18 (Kleiss' marked 2-S-18 and Donnell's 6-S-18). Realizing that he was in the wrong place, Donnell pulled up sharply and moved to his own sector. Kleiss completed his search in spite of the bad weather, but upon arriving at Point Option was unable to locate the ship. Heavy clouds prevented him from even seeing the ocean at 300 feet. Flying squares did not help, so he finally climbed for altitude, and managed to get a fix on the ship after an hour, and followed the prescribed course to the southeast for 150 miles. After another lengthy interval, with his gas gauge wobbling near empty, he finally spotted her through a tiny hole in the clouds. He dove straight down without flaps, and pulled out at 1,000 feet. Briefly under fire from *Enterprise*'s

screen until he established his friendly character, "Dusty" Kleiss and John Snowden came on board with less than 25 gallons of fuel remaining.

After conducting search and patrol operations well into the forenoon watch, meanwhile, *Enterprise*, screened by seven destroyers drawn from TF 1, headed for Pearl at 1100. The destroyers accompanying her had been chosen by RADM Draemel due to their short-handed condition—they had sortied in such haste that many officers and men had been unable to join the ships before they sailed.

LT(jg) Jim McCauley, among the pilots who flew an anti-submarine patrol ahead of the ship on the 8th, flew into Pearl that morning. Seeing the extensive damage and the "terrific mess," including *Arizona*, which still lay burning, made an indelible impression on him. "It was actually a pretty rugged thing to look at," he remembered, "not only from the obvious loss of life, but the fact that there stood our vaunted battle line of eight battleships . . ."

Enterprise entered Pearl Harbor at the start of the first dog watch (shortly after 1600) and moored, starboard side-to, in berth F-9, on the west side of Ford Island. Beholding the dismal devastation that lay before him, Halsey left no doubt of his feelings as Doug Moulton heard the admiral mutter: "Before we're through with 'em, the Japanese language will be spoken only in hell."

CDR Browning met VADM Halsey upon his arrival, and accompanied him as he called upon ADM Kimmel. *Enterprise*, meanwhile, received orders to fuel immediately and sortie at midnight, but due to what COMAIRBATFOR's war diary calls an "inexplicable error," the oiler *Neosho* (AO-23) did not moor alongside until 2300, delaying the carrier's sortie for four hours. The fueling operation proceeded apace, done "very smartly" in spite of the prevailing black-out conditions.

Halsey spent the intervening hours on shore at CINCPAC's headquarters where he found Kimmel's staff a dirty, unshaven bunch whose chins, however, "were well up in the air." He dined with the admiral

The heavy cruiser *Northampton* (CA-26) enters Pearl Harbor on the morning of 8 December 1941, her men observing the devastation wreaked by Japanese planes the previous day. From her bridge, RADM Raymond A. Spruance silently looked on, his reading and studying about war not having prepared him for the awful sight that lay before him. That evening, he emotionally and tearfully related his feelings to his wife and daughter. Apparently, though, he never spoke of it again.
(80-G-32548)

in his administrative spaces (a "damn poor" dinner, Halsey later recalled), during which time Kimmel received a report of paratroopers and gliders landing at Fort Weaver. Hearing that, Halsey guffawed. Kimmel growled: "What in the hell are you laughing at?"

"I have heard many damn fool reports in my life," Halsey replied, composing himself, "but without exception that is the damnest fool one I have ever heard. The Japs are not using their precious carrier decks to take off paratroopers and gliders," COM-AIRBATFOR declared, "and it is not possible for them to tow gliders from the nearest base to Oahu because of the distance . . ." Kimmel agreed.

While *Enterprise* lay at Pearl, taking on fuel and stores, her air group based on shore. Bombing SIX went to Hickam, where her pilots spent a sleepless night slapping mosquitoes in an old wooden temporary barracks. The Army base had taken "quite a pasting" from the Japanese on the 7th, and after dark one took one's life into one's own hands to move around. Rumors of blue-clad paratroops landing on Oahu on the 7th had prompted Bombing SIX's of-

ficers to look out for their enlisted men. "The rumor," Jim McCauley stated, "was that the Japs had been wearing blues and that was the uniform to shoot at..." On the night of the 8th, the rumored landing of Japanese paratroops at Fort Weaver—undoubtedly the same one that prompted Halsey's mirth at Kimmel's headquarters—brought an anxious request to LCDR William R. Hollingsworth, Bombing SIX's CO, to take some planes up to deal with the enemy. Hollingsworth told him that such a task was an "impossibility," and that it was up to the infantry to take care of the glider troops, not Bombing SIX! As it turned out, Halsey and Hollingsworth were right: the glider report was ludicrous. The 14th Naval District Control Post Watch Officer's Log noted at 2342 on the 8th: "Forts Weaver and Kam[ehameha] report that glider troops reports were in error, caused by confusion over [a] PBY landing."

Fighting SIX, meanwhile, had gone to Wheeler Field, placed under the Army's Interceptor Command. Due to mud in the revetments, the squadron's F4Fs had had to be dispersed on the concrete apron, while the pilots slept—or, rather, tried to—in private quarters that had been vacated by their previous occupants. Sporadic machine gun and rifle fire, though, kept many from getting a good night's sleep that night.

The Japanese raid the previous morning had destroyed the regular mess halls, necessitating the establishment of emergency facilities. "Wonder how those Japs knew where the Mess Halls were?" mused

The destroyer *McCall* stands up the dry dock channel early on the afternoon of 8 December. In the background (L-R) lie the light cruiser *Helena* (CL-50), the submarine *Cachalot* (SS-170) (behind a covered lighter) and *Pennsylvania*. In upper left background is that prominent Hawaiian landmark, Diamond Head. (80-G-32502)

View from the water tower at NAS Pearl Harbor, 8 December 1941; in front of hangars at top left are three SBDs from the *Enterprise* Air Group. Various utility aircraft sit scattered around the mat in foreground, including some whose wings appear to have been hastily camouflaged. Identifiable ships include the seaplane tender *Tangier* (AV-8), heavy cruiser *Chester* (CA-27), the damaged light cruiser *Raleigh* (CL-7) and the hospital ship *Solace* (AH-5). (80-G-32482)

one VF-6 pilot, "They [the enemy] not only play dirty, but fight dirty when they take away a man's chow." Diligent searching, though, managed to locate "a small quantity of bottled goods," as Fighting SIX's diarist put it: "With all that shooting going on outside, a fellow needs something refreshing." "It was anything but comforting," he continues, "to know that we had to hike down to our planes before daybreak with all that steel flying around." Woe betide the man who failed to respond with the countersign "Valley Forge" when someone in the darkness challenged them with "Washington."

Enterprise sortied from Pearl the following morning, and her air group rejoined her once out at sea, all hands glad to be back on board. Submarine contacts proliferated, and *Benham* depth-charged one a short time after TF 8 had sortied from Pearl. Over the next few days, the fleet picked up the pieces after the Pearl Harbor attack. Likewise, so did the *Enterprise* Air Group after its harrowing baptism of fire. Her pilots continued to fly searches and saw more whitecaps and clouds, but some experienced more than the routine. On 10 December, a succession of three VB-6 pilots reported a submarine at 0615, 0617 and 0940, operating nearby; two dropped 1,000-pound bombs. Perry Teaff, flying the group commander's SBD-2, sighted an I-boat early that afternoon and bombed her just after she had submerged.

Using the 0615 sighting as his starting point, "Dick" Dickinson, flying 6-B-1 with Tom Merritt as his radio-gunner, during the afternoon search, sighted what was probably the same submarine. At 1,800 feet to start with, Dickinson climbed for altitude, reaching between 4,500 and 5,000 feet before the I-boat apparently sighted him and opened fire with machine guns. Pushing over into a 65-degree dive, he released his bomb at 1,700 feet. It landed about 30 feet to port and 10 feet ahead of the conning tower; the submersible sank "in a vertical manner" with no forward motion. Dickinson saw a large oil slick and a few bubbles. Postwar accounting revealed the victim to be *I-70*, LCDR Takao Sano commanding.

Throughout the afternoon, *Enterprise*'s screen reported numerous sound contacts, with the carrier maneuvering accordingly. *Balch* developed two depth charge attacks on contacts she obtained. An error in radar reporting, coupled with an "inaccurate report from [the] battle lookouts," prompted immediate concern over a developing air attack. Fortunately, the "enemy" planes turned out to be "friendly" aircraft of the inner air patrol!

On Kauai, meanwhile, a LTCOL E.J. Fitz Gerald, USA, asked "Pat" Patriarca—who'd been released from hospital on 10 December (his whereabouts made known to the 14th Naval District Intelligence Officer by LCDR James W. Baldwin, USNR, on Kauai)—to undertake a "reconnaissance hop" around the island on the 11th. Complying, Patriarca took 6-S-16 up by himself, without his radio-gunner, and flew the requested mission. Upon his return, however, while he landed safely, he taxied too close to the obstructions placed near the runway, and his starboard wing hit a tar barrel. The SBD-3P's wingtip crumpled and the plane stood on its nose, bending the propeller beyond repair. An inter-island airliner subsequently brought Patriarca and DeLuca back to Oahu none the worse for wear from their sojourn on Kauai. They both rejoined their squadron, as "Dusty" Kleiss later recounted: "After being given up as dead and all their gear packed and their names about to be scratched off, they reappeared a week later without a scratch and with wild tales about their experiences with Jap fighters and cracking up [the] plane in obstruction barrels at Burns Field. Pat said the devil sent him back because 'Pat could raise more hell up there than I can down here.'" DeLuca had been moved from place to place with his machine gun, accompanied by the soldier assigned to carry his ammunition. The Army made him a tripod on which he could mount the Browning the second day he was there. If the Japanese had attempted a landing on Kauai on the 7th—as indeed everyone feared—DeLuca was to have cradled the gun in his arms and fired from the hip, "just like Victor McLaglen."

LCDR Young, LCDR Hopping, and all of the surviving pilots of the a.m. search (except the hospitalized Charlie McCarthy) soon recorded their experiences of that eventful morning and the days afterward. Hopping praised the conduct of his men as "in keeping with the highest traditions of the Navy." Separated into small two-plane units, no one had any knowledge of the developing situation on Oahu "until in the landing approach lanes." Hopping believed that all adopted the same course of action: try to land, obtain bombs, insure that Commander, TF 8, was kept fully informed of what was happening locally, and then "be prepared to search for and attack the Japanese raiding force."

Hopping singled out four of his men—three officers and one enlisted man—as "worthy of special commendation," and each received appropriate awards. Dickinson was awarded a Navy Cross for his performance of duty on the 7th (and a second for his sinking *I-70*). Perry Teaff was awarded a Navy Cross for his continuing on with a defective engine to search for the enemy. Ed Deacon was commended by the Secretary of the Navy for "distinguished devotion to duty, unusual presence of mind, and extra-

Mrs. Melvin B. Miller, mother of the late William C. Miller, christens the ship named for her brave son, smashing a bottle of Friar's New York State domestic champagne on her bow, at the Boston Navy Yard at 1630, 2 July 1943. (NH 102147)

William C. Miller (DE-359), *circa* 1945. (NH 78754)

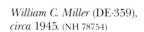

Willis (DE-395), underway in 1944. Note high-frequency direction finder antenna atop her foremast. (USN)

ordinary courage and disregard of his own safety" in the rescue of his radioman from his crashed plane. Dickinson's gallant radioman, Miller, was commended posthumously for heroism by the Secretary of the Navy, and a destroyer escort, *William C. Miller* (DE-259), was named for him.

The ship amply avenged Miller's loss, earning seven battle stars in World War II and destroying the Japanese submarine *I-6* on 14 July 1945. Fittingly, *William C. Miller* was present in Tokyo Bay during the surrender ceremony on 2 September 1945. *Willis* (DE-395) honored the Scouting SIX pilot, and earned one battle star for service in the Atlantic theater, as well as a share of the Presidential Unit Citation awarded the task group formed around the escort carrier *Bogue* (CVE-9). The Navy honored the memory of ENS Menges by naming a destroyer escort for him, too. Manned by a Coast Guard crew, *Menges* (DE-320) earned two battle stars for her service in the Atlantic. Torpedoed by *U-371* on 3 May 1944, she eventually reentered service, her shattered stern replaced by that taken from her sister ship *Holder* (DE-401).

The Hopping "Goes Down to the Sea"

The destroyer-escort U. S. S. Hopping slides into the Elizabeth River after her launching here Tuesday, March 9. Inset shows C. R. Warren, chief quarterman in the Inside Machine Shop (31) presenting Mrs. Hallsted L. Hopping, sponsor of the ship and for whose late husband, Lieut. Commander Hopping, the vessel is named, with a memento of the occasion, a gift from Yard employees.

U. S. S. Hopping Goes Down Ways and It's More Bad News For Axis Submarines

Christened by the wife of Lieutenant Commander Hallsted L. Hopping, a naval pilot who lost his life in action in the Pacific last year, the Navy Yard launched the destroyer-escort U. S. S. Hopping Tuesday, March 9, adding another weapon to the Navy's offensive against the Axis U-boats.

The Hopping was sent down the ways with little ceremony. Admiral Gygax presented the sponsor, Mrs. Hopping, who crashed the champagne bottle against the prow of the vessel with the words, "I hope this ship will play a part in making the world a better place for my child and all others."

The Hopping will bristle with guns when she is commissioned and puts out to sea to seek out the enemy and destroy him. She was built in near-record time and is a tribute to the men and women who built her, working at times in bitterly cold weather.

Tokyo, Rome and Berlin marked down "bad news" on their much-publicized "timetable" when the Hopping slid down the ways, for this trim little ship is one of many the Navy has ordered built to wipe the Axis submarines from the seas once and for all.

Formal photograph of LCDR Hallsted Lubeck Hopping, CO of VS-6. His widow presented a copy of this portrait to the ship named in his honor when she was commissioned on 21 May 1943. (NH 49242)

Excerpt from the front page of the Norfolk Navy Yard paper, March 17, 1943, recounting the launch of the destroyer escort *Hopping*. (*Hopping* Ship Name and Sponsor File)

The war continued, and took a toll not only of the men who flew into Pearl at the conclusion of the a.m. search on the morning of 7 December, but of those who survived the antiaircraft fire over the harbor when "Fritz" Hebel's flight sought safe haven at Ford Island that night.

Hopping—the first USN squadron commander to be lost in action in World War II—and his radiogunner, Harold "R" Thomas, were among the first to die, shot down in the attack on the Marshall Islands on 1 February 1942; Carl Fogg and Otis Lee Dennis perished in the same battle. Posthumous citations honored both pilots, as did ship names—*Hopping* (APD-51), a high speed transport converted from a destroyer escort, and *Fogg* (DE-57)—while the Navy honored Carl Fogg's radioman in like manner. *Dennis* (DE-405) earned four battle stars and a share of the Presidential Unit Citation awarded "Taffy THREE" for its valiant fight with four Japanese battleships and five heavy cruisers off Samar, in the Battle for Leyte Gulf. During one phase of the action, she rescued 434 survivors of the kamikazied *St. Lo* (CVE-63). *Dennis* later distinguished herself off Okinawa, rescuing 88 men from the kamikaze-damaged *Sangamon* (CVE-26).

Over Taroa, in the Marshalls, a Japanese fighter shot up Bud Kroeger's SBD, putting him out of action until Midway. Perry Teaff suffered the loss of his right eye on 24 February 1942, the day of the Wake Island strike, when his SBD lost power during the predawn takeoff and crashed into the sea off *Enterprise*'s port bow. The destroyer *Blue* (DD-387) recovered Teaff, but despite almost an hour's search, never found Jinks. Japanese antiaircraft fire claimed

Dale Hilton and Jack Leaming's plane at Marcus on 4 March; both men spent the rest of the war in a POW camp, surviving their ordeal. "Bucky" Walters, along with his radioman, failed to return from a search on 13 May; neither man was ever seen again. Willy West perished in an airplane crash at sea on 20 May, drowning when his leg became entangled in the plane's radio antenna as it sank. An operational mishap likewise claimed Gayle Hermann on 25 May, when his F4F spun into the sea after taking off from *Enterprise*, and he drowned. At Midway on 4 June, Fred Weber, Lee Keaney, and Lou Hansen were among the missing in action. Weber, awarded a posthumous Navy Cross for his performance at Midway, had a destroyer escort (later converted to a high speed transport) named for him; *Weber* (APD-75) was awarded one battle star for her World War II service.

"Dobby" Dobson ended the war commanding his own squadron, VF-86, on board *Wasp* (CV-18). For him, the war came full circle; in the waning moments of the conflict, while flying a Grumman "Hellcat," he shot down the last Japanese plane to attack TF 38.

The men who took off from *Enterprise* on the a.m. search on 7 December 1941 faced not only a determined foe but friendly fire alike in the skies over Oahu. Those who managed to land went aloft again and, groping through the "fog of war," sought the enemy who had struck so devastatingly at Pearl Harbor. Though success eluded them, the fault was not theirs and in no wise diminishes their bravery. They had acquitted themselves well, and displayed an abundance of "steady nerves and stout hearts."

NOTES

Chapter I

Sources for this chapter include TF 8 War Diary; deck logs for *Enterprise, McCall* and *Sonoma*; Halsey MSS; Lundstrom, *The First Team*; Daniels and Rawie diaries and "War Record of Fighting Squadron Six" (hereinafter VF-6 diary); Best, Troemel, Kleiss, Hilton and Anderson; plans of the day and Battle Order No.1 wording from copies of those documents in the Kleiss diary. The story of John Vogt's spotting a small fleet of ships apparently originated as a rumor (note misspelled name, "Voight") recounted in the VF-6 "diary," one of the sources used by Edward P. Stafford in *The Big E*. As can be seen, it was Willis (not Vogt) who sighted "three small ships in column" (not a small fleet) during his search on 4 December. Vogt's roommate on board *Enterprise*, Ben Troemel, also confirmed that it was not Vogt who made the sighting. The reasons for Gonzalez' switching places with Anderson on the a.m. search is from Anderson. The passenger list for *Lurline* was published in the 5 December 1941 edition of the Honolulu *Star-Bulletin*. The order for the PBY operations along the route of TF 8 is contained in *Pearl Harbor Attack: Hearings before the Joint Committee on the Investigation of the Pearl Harbor Attack* (hereinafter PHA), Pt.17, p.2487.

Chapter II

Information on each officer in the a.m. search comes from biographical files in the Operational Archives Branch, and in the Ships' Histories Branch, Ship Name and Sponsor Files for *Willis, Hopping, Fogg, Dennis* and *Weber*. Information on Miller's marriage plans is from Ship Name and Sponsor File for *William C. Miller*. Individuals who contributed comments on their shipmates include: Best, Coslett, Deacon, DeLuca, Gallaher, Hilton, Kleiss, Kroeger, Leaming, Patriarca, and Snowden. Dickinson, *The Flying Guns*. For the events of 7 December 1941 at the entrance to Pearl Harbor: the reports of ENS Tanner, *Antares* and *Ward*; Outerbridge; radio log for Bishop's Point Section Base (which contains the text of Outerbridge's two messages) in PHA, Pt. 17, p. 2719. For the events at the Opana Station, see PHA Pt. 19, pp. 2966-2968.

Chapter III

Thresher and *Litchfield* logs; TF 8 War Diary and CTF 8 to CINCPAC, "Operations of Task Force EIGHT on 7 December 1941," plan of the day from Kleiss diary; Statements of the encounters with Japanese planes by the men from the a.m. search are contained in COMAIRBATFOR to CINCPAC, "Reports of Action with Japanese Air Force [sic] at Oahu, T. H., December 7, 1941 . . ." (narratives by Young, Hopping, Teaff, Dickinson, Fogg, Hilton, Kroeger, Dobson, Gallaher, West, Deacon, Roberts, Patriarca and Weber). Halsey MSS and his testimony given at the Hart Inquiry into the Pearl Harbor attack,

in PHA Pt. 26; Bryan, *Admiral Halsey's Story* and the Halsey MSS; Best; Kleiss, Daniels and VF-6 diaries; Shoemaker; Leaming to RJC; Erickson; MAG-21 "Record of Events," in "History of Marine Corps Air Station, Ewa . . ." and Larkin testimony in PHA Pt. 23, p. 713; Vogt's probable fate comes from Larkin testimony and PHA Pt. 19, 3633. Dickinson, *The Flying Guns; Pyro* report; Broadcast Schedule for KGU and KGMB is from the 6 December 1941 issues of the Honolulu *Star-Bulletin* and *Honolulu Advertiser*; BuAer "Trouble Report" dealing with the loss of 6-B-3 (BuNo 2181), Xerox copy provided by Dave Lucabaugh—it is believed that the wording of Gonzalez' transmissions (his second message, about the rubber boat, is rarely, if ever, mentioned in most accounts) recounted herein is the most accurate. COMAIRBATFOR files (RG 313) dealing with the loss of the SBDs; RJC interviews with Kleiss, Gallaher, Patriarca, and Deacon; Coslett to RJC; Roberts, "Air Raid Pearl Harbor . . ." Reports of the Army AA Units in PHA Pt. 18, pp.3016-3017.

Chapter IV

Kleiss, Daniels and VF-6 diary; information on the number of operational aircraft in Scouting SIX comes from "Task Organization and Availability of Pilots and Aircraft of Scouting Squadron SIX for Sunday, 7 December, 1941," (6 December 1941) in Kleiss diary; Daniels; narratives by the pilots mentioned; Leaming; Dickinson's odyssey to reach Ford Island is from *The Flying Guns* and Lord, *Day of Infamy*, the latter proving particularly valuable in pinning down the identity of the people who gave the downed pilot a lift; Dobson diary; CTF 8 "Report of Operations..." which includes reports by *Northampton, Chester* and *Salt Lake City* on their SOC operations on the 7th; RJC interviews with Patriarca and DeLuca; Erickson; the full identity of Dickinson's volunteer radio-gunner became known by reference to the VP-22 muster roll.

Chapter V

CTF 8 "Report of Operations . . ." details the encounter of the *Northampton* SOCs with the *Kaga* "Zero," identified as such because of the red fuselage mark reported on the attacking plane—distinctive markings for that ship; Best; Walters' report in COMAIRBATFOR to CINCPAC, "Reports of Action with Japanese Air Force . . ."; Kleiss diary; information on the six VF-6 pilots comes from biographical files in the Operational Archives; TF 8 War Diary; Dobson diary; McCauley statement and "Vivid Memories," VF-6, Kleiss and Daniels diaries; Daniels' "The Tragedy of VF-6 at Pearl Harbor," COMAIRBATFOR files (RG 313) dealing with the loss of the VF-6 planes; Lundstrom; William R. Roberts' Navy Cross citation; Daniels; Prange, *December 7, 1941 . . ., Vireo* report; Norwood to RJC; Honolulu *Star-Bulletin* 9 December 1941; NAS Kaneohe History; Troemel; Walters' comments about his landing at Kaneohe come from Burns, *Then There Was One*; Bellinger's warning to ships and Army AA units comes from 14th Naval District Control Post Watch Officer's Log, War Diary, PHA, Pt. 24, p. 1650; Mason, *Battleship Sailor*, p. 242. *The Big E* contains an account (no source identified) of a torpedo coming loose from one of the TBDs (the barrier crash recorded in *Enterprise*'s log?)—an event not recorded in any contemporary primary (or secondary) source.

Chapter VI

TF 8 War Diary, VF-6 diary; CTF 8 "Report of Operations," Best; Kleiss diary; McCauley statement and "Vivid Memories," Halsey's reaction to the report of "gliders" and "paratroops" comes from his MSS autobiography; the confusion over the PBY landing that prompted the erroneous report is recorded in PHA, Pt.24, p. 1651. Navy Cross citations¹ for Dickinson and Teaff, and Deacon's commendation, from Awards Files, Ships' Histories Branch; information on Miller's commendation from *William C. Miller* Ship Name and Sponsor File. Information on the ships' World War II careers from the Source Files for the relevant warships in the Ships' Histories Branch.

SOURCES

I) List of Participants Consulted

CAPT Edward L. Anderson (VB-6)
RADM William H. Ashford, Jr. (Staff, COMAIRBATFOR)
LCDR Richard H. Best (VB-6)
Allen Brost (VB-6)
CWO3 Audrey G. Coslett (VS-6)
CAPT Edward T. Deacon (VS-6)
CDR Joseph F. DeLuca (VS-6)
RADM Wilmer E. Gallaher (VS-6)
CAPT H. Dale Hilton (VS-6)
CAPT Norman J. Kleiss (VS-6)
CAPT Edwin J. Kroeger (VB-6)
Jack Leaming (VS-6)
CDR James Murray (VB-6)
J. Lamont Norwood (*Vireo*)
RADM William W. Outerbridge (*Ward*)
CAPT Frank A. Patriarca (VS-6)
RADM Wilmer E. Roberts (VB-6)
LCDR John Snowden (VS-6)

II) Documents
a) Action Reports in the Operational Archives Branch, Naval Historical Center, Washington, D.C.

COMAIRBATFOR (VADM William F. Halsey, Jr.) to CINCPAC "Reports of Action with Japanese Air Force [sic] at Oahu, T. H., December 7, 1941, and with Submarine on December 10, 1941" (2 January 1942) (includes narratives by Young, Hopping, Teaff, Dickinson, Fogg, Hilton, Kroeger, Dobson, Gallaher, West, Deacon, Roberts, Patriarca and Weber).

CO, *Antares* (AKS-3) to CINCPAC, "Air Raid on Oahu December 7, 1941; Report on" (10 December 1941)

CO, *Argonne* (AG-31) to CINCPAC, "U.S.S. ARGONNE (AG31)—Enemy Attack, December 7, 1941; Detailed report of" (28 January 1942)

CO, *Neosho* (AO-23) to CINCPAC, "Raid on Pearl Harbor, T.H., December 7, 1941—Report on," (11 December 1941)

CO, *Pyro* (AE-1) to CINCPAC, "Japanese Air Attack on Sunday, 7 December 1941—Report of," (10 December 1941)

CO, *Ward* (DD-139) to COM 14, "Sinking of a Japanese Submarine by USS Ward" (13 December 1941)

CTF 8 (VADM Halsey) to CINCPAC, "Operations of Task Force EIGHT on 7 December 1941" (18 December 1941)

ENS William P. Tanner, A-V(N), USNR to CO, VP-14, "Narrative of Engagement with enemy submarine on December 7, 1941." (28 January 1942) as Enclosure "A" to CO, VP-14 to COMPATWING TWO, "Pilot's Reports of engagements with the enemy on December 7, 1941—Forwarding of," (28 January 1942)

b) Reports in the Prange Papers

5th Carrier Division Detailed War Report No. 1, (*Shokaku* and *Zuikaku*), Hawaii Assault Operation in the 1st Period of the 1st Stage Operations (8 December 1941) (English Translation)

Yokosuka Naval Air Corps, Air Branch Committee, Battlelessons Investigation Committee, "Lessons (Air Operation) of the Sea Battle off Hawaii, Vol. I," (*circa* August 1942) (English Translation)

c) War Diaries in the Operational Archives Branch, Naval Historical Center

TF 8 (COMAIRBATFOR) (28 November 1941-31 December 1941)

d) Ship Source Files; Name and Sponsor Files, Ships' Histories Branch, Naval Historical Center
Dennis (DE-405)
Fogg (DE-57)
Hopping (APD-51)
Menges (DE-320)
Weber (APD-75)
William C. Miller (DE-259)
Willis (DE-395)

e) Deck Logs in the National Archives' Military Reference Branch, Records of the Bureau of Navigation (RG 24), Washington, D.C.
Enterprise (CV-6) (29 November-11 December 1941)
Thresher (SS-200) (6-7 December 1941)
Litchfield (DD-336) (6-7 December 1941)
McCall (DD-400) (5-7 December 1941)
Nevada (BB-36) (7 December 1941)
Pennsylvania (BB-38) (7 December 1941)
Sonoma (AT-12) (1-7 December 1941)

f) Muster Rolls in the National Archives' Military Service Branch, Washington, D.C.
VP-22

g) Reports in National Archives' Military Reference Branch, U.S. Fleet, Records of Naval Operating Forces (RG 313), COMAIRBATFOR files
District Intelligence Field Unit, Navy Yard, Pearl Harbor, to Naval Air Station Field Unit, "U.S. Navy Plane shot down in Gulch near Wheeler Field" (26 December 1941) w/ enclosures
Officer-in-Charge, Intelligence Field Unit, NAS Pearl Harbor, to District Intelligence Officer, "Burned American Plane on Pearl City Peninsula," (14 December 1941)
Structures Officer for Aircraft to CO, USS *Enterprise*, "Location of Missing Aircraft," (29 December 1941)
Structures Officer for Aircraft to Commander Scouting Squadron SIX, "Missing Aircraft," (1 January 1942)

h) Interviews, Statements and Memoranda
CAPT Edward T. Deacon, USN (Ret.), Rockville, Maryland, 17 July 1987

LT Clarence E. Dickinson, Interview in the Bureau of Aeronautics, Washington, D. C., 10 July 1942. (Operational Archives Branch)
LT Frank Erickson, USCG (undated) (in USCGC *Taney* File, Coast Guard Historian's Office, Washington, D.C.)
RADM Wilmer E. Gallaher, USN (Ret.), 1 February 1983 (RJC Telephone Interview)
CDR James W. McCauley, USN, "Statement," 24 June 1945 (Operational Archives Branch)
CAPT Frank A. Patriarca, USN (Ret.), 6 August 1986 (RJC Telephone Interview)
CAPT Norman J. Kleiss, USN (Ret.), 20 April 1987 (RJC Telephone Interview)
CAPT Norman J. Kleiss, USN (Ret), Berkeley Springs, West Virginia, 5 May 1987
CAPT James M. Shoemaker, USN, "Memorandum for File . . . Japanese Air Raid on 7 December [1941]," dtd. 22 December 1941, in ADM Claude C. Bloch Papers, Library of Congress Manuscript Division, Washington, D. C. (SA-SL Miscellaneous, Box 3)

i) Letters
Edward L. Anderson to RJC, May 1987
Richard H. Best to RJC, 22 March 1987
Audrey G. Coslett to RJC, September 1987
Cleo J. Dobson to Walter Lord, 18 April 1956 (furnished by Mrs. Dobson)
H. Dale Hilton to RJC,
Jack Leaming to RJC, May 1987
Frank Kozelek to RJC, 17 May 1987
J. Lamont Norwood to RJC, 31 October 1988
William W. Outerbridge to RJC, 6 January 1975
Wilber E. Roberts to RJC,
John Snowden to RJC, June 1987
Benjamin H. Troemel to RJC, 7 March 1987

j) Miscellaneous
SS *Pat Doheny* Record Card, Convoy and Routing Files, Operational Archives Branch, Naval Historical Center, Washington, D. C.

III) Unpublished Diaries and Manuscripts

a) Personal Diaries
LT(jg) James G. Daniels, III (November-December 1941) (furnished by John Lundstrom)
LT(jg) Norman J. Kleiss (December 1941, with enclosures) (furnished by CAPT Kleiss)

ENS Cleo J. Dobson, "War Diary," (December 1941) (furnished by Mrs. Jane Dobson)

LT(jg) Wilmer E. Rawie (November-December 1941) (furnished by John Lundstrom)

"The War Record of Fighting Six, December 7, 1941 to June 21, 1942," presented by CDR James S. Gray, Jr., to the U.S. Naval Academy

b) Manuscripts

William F. Halsey, Jr., "Life of Admiral W.F. Halsey" (unpub. MSS), (Virginia Historical Society, Richmond)

Wilbur E. Roberts, "Air Raid, Pearl Harbor X This is No Drill," (unpub. MSS, furnished to RJC by RADM Roberts)

United States Marine Corps, "History of Marine Corps Air Station, Ewa, Oahu, T. H., 1941-1944," (Reference Section, Marine Corps Historical Center)

United States Naval Air Station, Kaneohe Bay, "History," (1 August 1939-1 August 1945) (Operational Archives Branch, Aviation History Files)

IV) Books

Buell, Thomas B., *The Quiet Warrior: A Biography of Admiral Raymond A. Spruance* (Boston: Little, Brown and Co., 1974)

Burns, Eugene, *Then There Was One: The U.S.S. Enterprise and the First Year of War* (New York: Harcourt, Brace and Co., 1944)

Dickinson, Clarence E., *The Flying Guns: Cockpit Record of a Naval Pilot from Pearl Harbor Through Midway*, in collab. with Boyden Sparkes (New York: Charles Scribner's Sons, 1942)

Halsey, William F., with J. Bryan,III, *Admiral Halsey's Story* (New York: Whittlesey House, 1947)

Japan: War History Office, *Senshi Sosho* (War History Series), Volume 10, *Hawai Sakusen* (Tokyo: Asagumo Shimbunsa, 1970)

Lord, Walter, *Day of Infamy* (New York: Henry Holt and Co., 1957)

Lundstrom, John B., *The First Team: Pacific Naval Air Combat from Pearl Harbor to Midway* (Annapolis: Naval Institute Press, 1984)

Mason, Theodore, *Battleship Sailor* (Annapolis: Naval Institute Press, 1982)

Prange, Gordon W., with Donald Goldstein and Kathleen V. Dillon, *At Dawn We Slept: The Untold Story of Pearl Harbor* (New York: McGraw-Hill, 1981)

_____ *December 7, 1941: The Day the Japanese Attacked Pearl Harbor* (New York: McGraw-Hill, 1988)

Stafford, Edward P., *The Big E* (New York: Random House, 1962)

U.S. Congress, 79th Congress, 1st Session, *Pearl Harbor Attack: Hearings before the Joint Committee on the Investigation of the Pearl Harbor Attack*. 39 parts. (Washington, DC: Government Printing Office, 1946)

V) Articles

Daniels, James G., "The Tragedy of VF-6 At Pearl Harbor," (Naval Aviation Museum) *Foundation* Vol. 7, No. 2 (Fall 1986)

Gray, James S., "Why Them and Not Me?", comments on, in "Comment and Discussion," *U.S. Naval Institute Proceedings* (December 1981)

Kaye, Harold S., "Hickam Field, 7 December 1941: The First U.S. Army Air Corps Flying Fortress (B-17D) Combat Mission in World War II," *Aerospace Historian*, Vol. 33, No. 4, Winter/December 1986.

McCauley, James W., "Vivid Memories," *Shipmate*, Vol. 47, No.10, (December 1984)

VI) Newspapers

Honolulu *Star-Bulletin*, 27 November-7 December 1941 (incl.)

Honolulu *Advertiser*, 27 November-7 December 1941 (incl.)

INDEX